Presented to

_____

By

_____

Date

_____

THE COMPLETE A-Z GUIDE
TO ONLINE MARKETING TERMS

INTERNET MARKETING
DICTIONARY

KIM FAITH

INTERNET MARKETING DICTIONARY

The Complete A-Z Guide to Online Marketing Terms
Copyright© 2015

Disclaimer

Published by
URBAN DESIGN LLC

TABLE OF CONTENTS

Foreword

A

B

C

D

E

F

G

H

I

J

K

L

M

N

O

P

Q

R

S

T

U

V

W

X

Y

Z

FOREWORD

Have you ever been in a conversation with someone who used so much technical jargon that you found yourself completely lost?

The internet marketing industry has a language of its own. The jumbled jargons of complete new words...in confusing terms...and acronyms in all shapes and forms which you will find commonly here and there nowadays.

Let's face it, the biggest problems with the marketing jargons is that, it doesn't make internet marketing easier. Isn't it frustrating and confusing when some marketing gurus just throw you jargons of words around casually and will expect you to know the language of its own? It's easy for miscommunications to happen when not everyone has the same vocabulary, and when you're trying to build your business, this can be a real problem.

And that is the reason why this book was created... we've compiled some of the marketing and advertising terms which many business owners don't already know, but which are essential to getting the most out of your marketing works, meetings, businesses and research. List of some of the most common online marketing terms you're likely to encounter, and some that you might not to make the introduction into marketing just that little bit easier for you.

And now here comes the product, a complete A-Z guide book to online marketing terms, Internet Marketing Dictionary.

A great daily companion book for all web browsers and internet marketers!

If you enjoyed our complete A-Z guide to online marketing terms, or you think we've missed something, kindly please feel free to let us know in the Amazon's comment section.

As we're always adding new terms to keep marketers up to date in the ever-evolving marketing profession, I'd be very grateful if you'd post a short review on Amazon. Your support really does make a difference to make this book even better.

Thanks again for your support!

A

ABANDONMENT - The discontinuance of a marketed product. It is also called product deletion or product elimination. Abandonment may occur at any time from shortly after launch (a new product failure) to many years later. The criterion for this decision is the same as for a new product: net present value of the product's estimated stream of future earnings, both direct and indirect.

ABANDONMENT RATE - The abandonment rate is related to the use of online shopping carts and how often the sales are abandoned rather than completed. Many people start the checkout process, but don't complete the transaction by making a purchase. This is called "abandonment". It's useful information for marketers, who can use it to figure out how many shopping carts used in a specified time results in a completed sales versus shopping carts that are abandoned, i.e. On Saturdays there are higher abandonment rates than on Fridays. And just so you know, the average abandonment rate is 48.50%.

ABC ANALYSIS - An approach for classifying accounts based on their attractiveness. Accounts are the most attractive while C accounts are the least attractive.

ABC INVENTORY CLASSIFICATION - A classification scheme used to implement inventory management strategies. Products are segmented into groups based upon unit sales or some other criterion.

ABOUT.COM - Formerly known as The Mining Company, About is a guide based information portal.

ABOVE THE FOLD – Above the fold refers to banner advertisements which are displayed at the top of a web page. In general terms, "above the fold" means someone or something that goes above and beyond; in internet marketing terms it means the advertisement is above the entire page, or is the first thing people see when reaching the page.

ABOVE THE LINE COST - Any cost involved in the advertising production process that is specifically listed in the budget.

ABSOLUTE ADVANTAGE - When a country has the capacity to produce goods at a lower cost than another country, it is said to have an absolute production advantage. Even if a country has an absolute advantage in the production of all goods, it can still gain from specialization and trade if it has a comparative advantage in the production of any good.

ABSOLUTE URL's LINK – Refers to the use of the full-path internet address

ACCELERATED DEVELOPMENT – It is the process of speeding up new product development process. Development can be accelerated in a number of ways, such as speeding up the development process, eliminating unnecessary steps, undertaking two or more development tasks in parallel, and eliminating or minimizing decision-making delays.

ACCELERATED PURCHASE - A sales promotion goal achieved when consumers or channel members purchase the product before the time they would have normally bought.

ACCEPTABLE PRICE RANGE - Refers to the prices that buyers are willing to pay for goods or services.

ACCESSORIES - The miscellaneous apparel related items that are offered in department stores and apparel specialty stores including hosiery, jewelry, handbags, handkerchiefs, etc.

ACCOUNT - A customer, usually an institution or another organization, that purchases a company's products or services.

ACCOUNT CLASSIFICATION - The categorization of a salesperson's customers into groups, based on criteria such as potential sales, for the purpose of developing a sales call plan. Comment: The classification scheme reflects the relative attractiveness of the various customers and is used to direct sales effort.

ACCUMULATION - A sorting process that brings similar stocks from a number of sources together into a larger homogeneous supply.

ACQUISITION COST – The price it cost as business to gain a new customer, client, or supplier. The acquisition cost is the average cost per new customer for a business.

ACQUISITION STRATEGY – It is the process of finding potential customers who are in the market and ready to buy. The attempt to lead customers to a web site and to welcome them, answer their questions and close the sale.

ACQUISITION VALUE – Refers to the buyers' perceptions of the relative worth of a product or service to them. It is formally defined as the subjectively weighted difference between the most a buyer would be willing to pay for the item less the actual price of the item.

ACTIVATION - The essentially automatic process by which knowledge and meanings are retrieved from memory and made available for use by cognitive processes.

ADAPTATION PRICING POLICY - A pricing for the rest of the world of adapting home country prices to local competitive and market circumstances. It also is known as polycentric pricing policy.

AD – The name used to indicate an advertising message in the print media.

AD BLOCKING - Software available to internet users that blocks the appearance of advertising on Web pages. Typically, these programs suppress so-called pop-up and pop-under ads.

AD CLICKS - Refers to the number of times users click on an ad banner.

AD CENTER - Refers to Bing Ads which was formally known as Microsoft ad Center and is now the second largest paid search provider in the United States.

AD COPY – Writing that is specifically done for the advertisements. The ad copy is often another term for actual text within an ad. The better the ad copy, the more chances it will bring sales.

AD GROUPS – It refers to a group of ads within a campaign.

ADD-ON - In charge accounts, the purchasing of additional merchandise without paying in full for previous purchases, especially in installment-credit plan selling.

ADDRESS - A unique identifier for a computer or site online, usually a URL for a web site for marked with a @ for an email address. Literally, it is how your computer finds a location on the information highway.

AD ROTATION – When a web page shows a different ad at the top of the page each time it is viewed by a new person, or when the web page is refreshed.

AD SCHEDULING - In internet marketing, Ad Scheduling is the practice of scheduling the day into several parts, during each of which a different advertising rule is applied based on advertising objective, budget, and competitors.

AD SENSE _ Ad sense is one of Google's many goodies. It is an advertising system that provides website owners with the opportunity to generate income by placing Google ads on their page. Google sets up either text, image, video ads based on certain keywords within the site's context. The amount of money generated is in direct correlation to the amount of traffic that visits the site.

AD TITLE - The first line of text displayed in a clickable search or context-served ad. Ad Titles serve as ad headlines.

AD TRACKER - It refers to a software program that allows a website administrator to know which ads are getting traffic and which are not. It helps to gauge accurately the target audience, thus you can save money by knowing which ads are working.

AD TRACKING – A method used to check how many hits or clicks an ads receives, as well as the particular demographic that most people click on the ad. It is a useful tool for discovering where the most revenue comes from, and how to better personalize ads to reach more customers, and encourage more new customers via the ads published or produced.

ADVANCE DATING - An arrangement by which the seller sets a specific future date when the terms of sale become applicable.

ADVANCE ORDER - An order placed well in advance of the desired time of shipment. By placing orders in advance of the actual buying season, a buyer is enabled often to get a lower price because the buyer gives the supplier business when the latter would normally be receiving little.

ADVERTISEMENT - Any announcement or persuasive message placed in the mass media in paid or donated time or space by an identified individual, company, or organization.

ADVERTISERS – Paying parties who want their company's ad on another website.

ADVERTISING - The placement of announcements and persuasive messages in time or space purchased in any of the mass media by business firms, nonprofit organizations, government agencies, and individuals who seek to inform and/ or persuade members of a particular target market or audience about their products, services, organizations, or ideas.

ADVERTISING CAMPAIGN – It refers to a group of advertisements, commercials, and related promotional materials and activities that are designed to be used during the same period of time as part of a coordinated advertising plan to meet the specified advertising objectives of a client.

ADVERTISING CLAIM - A statement made in advertising about the benefits, characteristics, and/or performance of a product or service designed to persuade the customer to make a purchase.

ADVERTISING CONTRACT – It pertains to a contractual agreement between an advertiser and the operator of any form of advertising media for the purchase of specified types of advertising time or space.

ADVERTISING COPY – It refers to the verbal or written component of advertising messages.

ADVERTISING EFFECTIVENESS - An evaluation of the extent to which a specific advertisement or advertising campaign meets the objectives specified by the client.

ADVERTISING IDEA - The theme or concept that serves as the organizing thought for an advertisement. Ideas are used to dramatize the product-related information conveyed in advertising.

ADVERTISING MEDIA - The various mass media that can be employed to carry advertising messages to potential audiences or target markets for products, services, organizations, or ideas. These media include newspapers, magazines, direct mail advertising, Yellow Pages, radio, broadcast television, cable television, outdoor advertising, transit advertising, and specialty advertising.

ADVERTISING NETWORK – Business owners often work with other internet businesses to agree to post their ads. This is known as an advertising network. You may notice a website selling electronics has another company's ad on their site; this means they are part of an advertising network, working together. ; An Internet business model where advertisers go to one source to buy advertising on several Web sites at once through run-of-category and run-of-network buys.

ADVERTORIAL

An advertorial is a hybrid between an advert and an editorial article. It's essentially an advertisement that is stylized like an editorial article to provide customers information about a product.

ADVIEWS - Number of times an ad banner is downloaded and presumably seen by visitors. If the same ad appears on multiple pages simultaneously, this statistic may understate the number of ad impressions, due to browser caching.

ADWORDS – Google's advertising pay per click program that is quickly becoming one of the most popular forms of ad affiliate plans on the web. Adwords is Google's advertising service that is largely focused on the use of keywords. Through Adwords, a business can create an ad that is triggered to show up when internet users search for a specific keyword that the business has set. The ads then appear as "sponsored links" on Google's results pages, as well as Google's partners such as AOL and Ask.com.

AFFILIATE – The person participating in any one company's affiliate program. An affiliate is also sometimes referred to as a "publisher".

AFFILIATE FRAUD - A dishonest tactic used by affiliates in an affiliate marketing program to generate unearned, illegitimate income. For example, an affiliate in a pay-per-click advertising program repeatedly clicking on a link to generate commission income.

AFFILIATE LINK - It refers to a unique hyperlink that allows an affiliate to promote whatever the business they are affiliated with wants them to promote.

AFFILIATE MARKETING - Affiliate marketing is type of performance-based marketing strategy where merchants reward affiliates who create extra business through their marketing efforts. The reward that affiliates will get from their efforts varies, but the general idea stays the same. ; An online marketing strategy that involves revenue sharing between online advertisers/merchants and online publishers/salespeople. Compensation is typically awarded based on performance measures such as sales, clicks, registrations or a combination of factors.

AFFILIATE MERCHANT - The advertiser in an affiliate marketing relationship.

AFFILIATE NETWORK - An affiliate network is a third party that works as middle man between the merchant affiliate programs and the potential affiliates. The affiliate network helps to connect merchant affiliate programs and potential affiliates, and vice versa. This helps affiliates find appropriate affiliate programs more easily. It also helps the merchant reach a larger audience by promoting their affiliate programs.

AFFILIATE PROGRAM – A program where other people known as affiliates, agree to advertise for the sponsor's site. In return, they receive commission or residual payment. This is also known as word as word of mouth advertising, but it is done through a network of affiliates who assist the website in getting the word out.

AFFILIATED STORE - A store operated as a unit of a voluntary group or franchise group. Also, it may be a store controlled by another store but operated under a separate name.

AFTER SALES SUPPORT - The services offered by the selling firm after the sale has been made to promote goodwill, to ensure customer satisfaction, and develop customer loyalty.

AIDA – Acronym for Attention, Interest, Desire and Action; this is the motivating factor for advertisers and web businesses to get exposure.

AJAX - Stands for Asynchronous JavaScript and XML. Ajax is a programming language that allows for the updating of specific sections of content on a web page, without completely reloading the page.

ALEXA – Lesser known search engine, Alexa has a free toolbar that allows users to see traffic data and other important information, making it an excellent resource for those who utilize internet marketing.

ALGORITHM - To get a computer working, you have to write a computer program which should tell the computer what you want it to do step-by-step. An algorithm tells a computer how to execute a computer program. It is an ordered collection of computable operations.

ALT TAG - or "Alternative text", is text that is associated with an image. The purpose of the written text is to convey the essential information of what the image is. The alt tag isn't usually visible, but where images have been turned off (or where screen readers are used due to a visual impairment) they serve to provide the same information to the visitors. Not including alt tags, or including unhelpful alt tags, can be frustrating for visually impaired internet users.

ALT TEXT - HTML coding that provides an alternative text message when a non-textual element such as in image fails to display properly.

ALTA VISTA - A popular search engine. One of the first search engines originally owned by Digital and is now owned by Yahoo.

AMAZON –Current largest online retailer in the world. This is a massive internet marketplace where users can buy or sell nearly unlimited amount of goods.

ANALYTICS - is the information that is a result of the practice of analyzing and measuring data. It is the summary of this data, presented in different formats. Ensuring that you continually view and consider the information available through analytics will help you improve your website's performance and maximize the business in question's ROI.

ANCHOR TEXT – It refers to the visible, clickable text for a hyperlink. It is the highlighted piece of text that is hyperlinked so that when you click on it you follow the link to another webpage or another website. Search engines use anchor text to determine what the subject of your page.

ANIMATED GIF - A format for graphic images that incorporates several images rotated in sequence. This technique is typically used to convey additional information in a limited space such as a banner ad.

APACHE - Apache is a free, open-source web server software system that is pervasive on UNIX, Linux, and similar operating system types. It is also available for Windows and other operating systems. Google Analytics' admin system is powered by a variant of Apache.

API - Acronym for Application Programming Interface. This is a program that advertisers create to manage their SEM campaigns, bypassing the search engines' interfaces.

APPLE – A multi-national technology company based in Cupertino California. This company designs, develops and markets high end consumer's electronics.

APPLET - An application program written in Java which allows viewing of simple animation on web pages.

APPLICATION or APP – It refers to a small, often specific program that can be downloaded into mobile devices.

APPLICATION SERVICE PROVIDER (ASP) – The term used to describe companies that provide software or services to a network of customers on an ongoing basis. Customers pay for those services in a stream of smaller payments rather than simply purchasing software outright.

APRON - A form attached to an invoice or copy of purchase order in retail stores, containing details to check before payment. It is sometimes called a rider.

ARBITRAGE – It is the act of buying something and selling it almost immediately to take advantage of a difference in price in another market.

ARTICLES – Written articles that pertain to a particular subject or website. These articles can then be submitted in the form of e-books, web zines, or integrated into a website in order to get more exposure on web searches such as Google.com

ARTICLE MARKETING - Article marketing is when businesses write short articles relating to their company, business or their industry expertise as part of their marketing strategy. They then share them on article directories, where the business can link the article back to their website or blog.

ASP – Abbreviation for Active Server Pages, this is a technology developed by Microsoft that allows scripts to be integrated into web pages. It helps to allow information to be integrated into website via the use of forms, etc.

ARTIFICIAL INTELLIGENCE – Abbreviation for AI. An area of computer science concerned with designing smart computer systems. AI systems exhibit the characteristics generally associated with intelligence in human learning, reasoning, and solving problems.

ASSOCIATION PROGRAM – Another term for affiliate program, some websites use the term associate program instead. People often prefer to use the term associate, as it sounds somewhat more professional and higher level than affiliate.

ASCII - American Standard Code for Information Interchange.

ASK JEEVES - A Meta search engine that allows natural English quires. You can ask a question as you search.

ASTROTURFING - Refers to the process of creating fake grassroots campaigns. Astroturfing is often used specifically regarding review sites like Google Places, Yelp, Judy's Book and more. These fake reviews can be positive reviews for your own company or slander against your competitors. Not a good idea.

ATTACHMENT – Refers to any kind of file that is attached to a message or email.

ATTRIBUTION - Attribution is when you identify what user-actions contributed to the desired outcome (usually described as a "conversion") and then assigning a value to each user-action that lead to that conversion. For example, if someone decided to sign-up after reading a particular blog post, that specific blog post would be assigned (or attributed) the value that lead to the successful sign-up.

AUCTIONS – A method in which items are sold online in auction format, and often for a terrific price compared to the same items purchased directly from online retailers. In addition, buyers often find rare items and antiques via online auctions.

AUTO-RESPONDER – An automated message or reply sent to customers via email when they request information from a website. People who sign up for online newsletters will receive one acknowledging that they have signed up. The auto-responder is also used to serve as acknowledgement of a concern or complaint when customer service is contacted. It also includes contact information for the company via telephone.

AUTOMATED TELLER MACHINE (ATM) – It is a machine that allows use of special cards by consumers to make deposits, withdraw cash, or transfer funds among accounts via electronic funds transfer.

AUTOMATIC CHECKOUT MACHINE (ACM) – It refers to a system whereby customers have the opportunity to check themselves out of a store by scanning their purchases with the point-of-sale system, entering their customer identification card, and receiving clearance to exit the store.

AUTOMATIC OPTIMIZATION - Search engines identify which ad for an individual advertiser demonstrates the highest CTR (click-through rate) as time progresses, and then optimizes the ad serve, showing that ad more often than other ads in the same Ad Group/Ad Order.

AVATAR – It refers to 2- or 3-D customized computer representations of people; also referred to as "icons" or "buddy icons" used on Instant Messenger. It is an online virtual community.

AVERAGE RESPONSE VALUE - The average revenue value of each click, calculated as total revenue divided by total clicks.

B

B2B – A popular short cut for saying Business to Business. This term refers to the relationship between businesses that only offer goods or services to other businesses, and not to private customers or individuals. B2B (Business-to-business) is a transaction that happens between two businesses, such as a manufacturer and a wholesaler or wholesaler and a retailer.

B2C – Acronym for Business to Consumer. It means the business offers goods or services directly to the private consumer, and NOT to businesses. A business to consumer merchant is usually a retail based type of business that only provides services or products directly to the individual. B2C (Business-to-consumer) is a transaction that happens between a business and consumers. In this transaction, the consumer is the intended end-users of the business' products or services (this is where those "not for resale" stickers you find on products comes into play).

BABY BOOM - The period from the end of World War II until the early 1960s when the number of births increased significantly, resulting in a population surge characterized as "the baby boom generation."

BACKBONE - A high-speed line or series of connections that forms a large pathway within a network. The term is relative to the size of network it is serving. A Backbone in a small network would probably be much smaller than many non-Backbone lines in a large network.

BACKDOOR – Refers to undocumented method for gaining access to a particular program, webpage, service and or computer system.

BACKDOOR SELLING - Sales to ultimate consumers by wholesalers who hold themselves out to be sellers only to retailers.

BACK END – A very profitable item or product that is sold to customers who have typically already purchased thief first item and the back end product is a result of that lead purchase.

BACKLINKS - Backlinks are links on other pages that will direct consumers and search engines to your page. They're also referred to as "Inbound Links".

BAIT ADVERTISING - An alluring but insincere offer to sell whereby the advertiser does not intend to sell the advertised product at the advertised price; the purpose is to increase customer traffic. It also is called bait and switch advertising.

BAIT AND SWITCH - A deceptive sales practice whereby a low-priced product is advertised to lure customers to a store, where they are then induced to buy higher priced models by disparaging the less-expensive product.

BAIT AND SWITCH ADVERTISING - The advertising of a product or service at an unusually low price with an intention to switch the customer to a higher priced item when the customer comes to the store to buy the advertised item. This practice is illegal if customers find it difficult or impossible to buy the advertised item.

BALANCE SHEET METHOD - It is often referred to as the Ben Franklin method. An approach used by salespeople to gain commitment from a buyer by asking the buyer to think of the pros and cons of various alternatives.

BAN - Refers to a punitive action imposed by a search engine in response to being spammed. Can be an IP address of a specific URL. Also known as delisting.

BANDWIDTH – A term used to describe the amount of capacity of data transferring through communications channel. The amount of bandwidth often determines the speed of which a website functions when the user clicks on links.

BANNER – Advertising method in which the ad is placed along the top of a website or web page horizontally. This is known as a banner ad, and can be a simple single picture with words or have animation or video and sound.

BANNER AD - A banner ad is a rectangular graphic that's usually shown at the top or bottom of a web page. Usually, it extends across the full page width of the screen. The purpose of the banner is to have visitors of the host's website click on the advertisement that will then link them back to the advertiser's website. Banner ads aren't a particularly effective form of advertising.

BANNER BLINDNESS - This is a term referring to the tendency of the internet users to ignore banner ads.

BANNER EXCHANGE – A method in which the advertisers work together and allow each other to place their banner ad at the top of the other's website.

BAR CODE - An information technology application that uniquely identifies various aspects of product characteristics as well as additional information regarding delivery and handling instructions. The information is read by scanning devices and greatly increases the speed, accuracy, and productivity of the distribution process.

BITCOIN – It refers to a new type of digital currency which value system is unpredictable and is not backed up by any particular bank or government. It is often utilized by people who want to make online purchases anonymously so that the sale does not trace back to them.

BLACK HAT SEO - Black Hat SEO is the practice of using unethical techniques so that the page ranks higher in search engines. Examples of Black Hat SEO are keyword stuffing, invisible texts, page swapping and doorway pages.

BASIC RESELLS RIGHTS – These are granted when you obtain the right to resell something, however the people purchasing it from you do not have the ability to resell it at that point.

BLACKLIST - A list of Web sites that are considered off limits or dangerous. A Web site can be placed on a blacklist because it is a fraudulent operation or because it exploits browser vulnerabilities to send spyware and other unwanted software to the user.

BLACK HAT WEBSITE – This is a popular term for websites that do not utilize SEO keywords properly but instead stuff them or spam them with too many keywords, integrate poorly written articles into the site, or try to trick the web spiders in order to be at the top of the search rankings.

BLIND LINK – An advertisement or link that does not reveal its source or tell the person who clicks on it where it might lead. This is sometimes considered deceptive in the internet marketing world, but it is still commonly used.

BLIND TRAFFIC – The traffic that is generated to any given website as a result of people clicking URL that they are not sure where it will lead.

BLOCK or BLOCKING – It is a term used to describe Banning someone from a particular website.

BLOG – Short for web log, blogs and blogging have quickly become a popular way to communicate, but they are also an excellent tool for marketing. Blogs allow people to write their own personal experience and opinions on certain products or services in a more intimate tone. This often encourages readers to check out the business that has been mentioned, making it an equitable form of marketing online.

BLOGGING - The term "blog" is a shortened version of "weblog," a combination of the two words "web" and "log". A blog may be run by an individual or group of people. There are two main types of blogs: A personal blog and a business blog. Both will usually include entries relating to a variety of topics. These can be articles, critical commentary, photos, videos, descriptions of experiences or events etc. Blogging has become an important aspect of inbound marketing. It improves website traffic growth, conversion rates and industry expertise, among other things.

BITMAP – Also known as "BMP" or "bump." It refers to a type of images made up of pixilated grid format known as raster graphics.

BOOKMARK - A special link stored in a Web browser to a Web site. Internet Explorer uses the term "Favorites" instead of bookmark.

BOOK MARKING – The process of marking a website in your browser with the intention of visiting again. The term bookmarking is also used when in reference to social bookmarking site, where people post and share their favorite websites with one another.

BOT - Abbreviation for robot, also called a spider. It refers to software programs that scan the web. Bots vary in purpose from indexing web pages for search engines to harvesting e-mail addresses for spammers.

BOTTOM OF THE FUNNEL - The bottom of the funnel refers to the stage in the sales funnel where leads are about to become customers. Typically, they've already identified what they need, they have shopped around and have decided that what you have to offer will work best for them, and now they are very close to making a purchase. This is the time usually where the lead will ask for a demo, pricing information or a consultation, depending on the business. The bottom of the funnel does not end with a lead turning into a customer, but instead becomes about "retention". This means keeping your customers happy and satisfied with their product/service by creating informative content or by adding new features to a service etc.

BOUNCE RATE - The bounce rate is the percentage of people who leave a website after viewing only one page. A high bounce rate means that improvements to the website need to be made so that you can keep visitors there for longer.

BRAND AWARENESS - Brand awareness is the extent to which a person can recognize a brand and correctly link it back to a specific product. Brand awareness is essential, as customers are much less likely to purchase your product if they're not aware of it.

BRANDING – A highly or widely recognized brand image (Xerox or Apple are examples). Branding brings recognition and exposure to businesses.

BRANDING ADVERT – An advertisement that effectively used a branded image to acquire more business. For example, the Apple iPod is often referenced by the Apple logo which is widely recognized. These advertisements are easy to spot, and people usually quickly recognize them.

BRAND LOYALTY - The extent of the faithfulness of consumers to a particular brand, expressed through their repeat purchases, irrespective of the marketing pressure generated by the competing brands.

BROAD MATCH – When words can have many different meanings and be associated with several different things, this is known as a broad match.

BROWSER CACHING - To speed surfing, browsers store recently used pages on a user's disk. If a site is revisited, browsers display pages from the disk instead of requesting them from the server. As a result, server's under-count the number of times a page is viewed.

BROWSING - A term that refers to exploring an online area, usually on the World Wide Web.

BUM MARKETING – A new marketing process that involves advertising affiliate links and websites. More information can be found at www.bummarketingmethod.com

BUTTON – A small tool used on website or add that can lead to another link, or it can be used to submit information via a form, email newsletter sign up, or other method. Buttons can be plain or use detailed graphics.

BUTTON AD – Refers to a graphical advertising unit smaller than a banner ad. It is also called as tile-ad.

C

CACHE - Cache is a storage area for frequently accessed information. Retrieval of the information is faster from the cache than the originating source. There are many types of cache including RAM cache, secondary cache, disk cache, and cache memory to name a few.

CACHING - A computer process that stores Web files for later re-use. The purpose is to save the user time by displaying Web pages without needing to re-download graphics and other elements of the page.

CAI – Abbreviation for Computer Assisted Interviewing. It refers to the conduct of surveys using computers to manage the sequence of questions and in which the answers are recorded electronically through the use of the keyboard.

CANONICALIZATION - The process of picking the best URL when there are several choices; this usually refers to home pages.

CALL TO ACTION - A Call to Action (often abbreviated as CTA) is a piece of text or image that asks your potential customers, readers, leads and visitors to take action. It is literally a "call" to your intended audience to take a certain "action". It's your CTA that takes your "visitors" and tries to convert them into "leads". The action that you want people to take can vary widely, from downloading a book to signing up for a newsletter. A call to action can be placed anywhere, including on your website, at the end of a blog post or in an email. The location, color, wording, whitespace and design all have major impacts on how effective your call to action will be, so it's best to test changes and see how well they perform. Testing and split testing minor changes is a good way to figure out what works best for your website.

CAMPAIGN – The energy and time put into trying to get your marketing and products exposed.

CAMTASIA – Software that allows the user to make videos, particular if you plan to make them entirely on your PC.

CIA – Abbreviation for Cash In Advance. It refers to payment before receipt or delivery of goods or services. Used interchangeably with cash before delivery, and applies in the same instance as the latter.

CIM – Abbreviation for Computer Integrated Manufacturing. It is an approach to managerial control that focuses on the automated flow of information among participants in the stages of manufacturing.

COD – Abbreviation for Cash on Delivery. It is the practice of collecting for the price of the merchandise plus the relevant transportation charges. It is commonly referred to as C.O.D.

CWO – Abbreviation for Cash with Order. It refers to the seller demands that cash covering the cost of merchandise and delivery accompany the customer's order; cash before delivery and cash in advance apply similarly.

CGI – An abbreviation for Common Gateway Interface. This is a way for a web server through a particular application program. CGI is used in many different webs programming application such as Perl and Java, as well as several others.

CHANNEL DISTRIBUTION - Products often pass through a few businesses before it reaches its end customer. This is referred to as channel distribution. There are indirect and direct channels. An example of a direct channel would be when a consumer can purchase straight from the manufacturer. An example of indirect channels would be when the product is purchased from a manufacturer by a wholesaler, and then a retailer purchases it, and finally, the consumer. Indirect channels are considered "longer" and manufacturer's run the risk of gaining less profit from their product, as fees or commissions are taken from the sale to pay the wholesaler. Direct channels are considered "shorter" but limit the amount of ways a customer can buy a product.

CLASSIFIED – Much like a newspaper classified ad, this term means text only ads online. It is usually offered for a free or a very small fee to Internet advertisers and can usually be found as part of a larger website or online magazine.

CLICKBANK – A payment processing service similar to PayPal. Click bank is often used for online services such as an internet provider, ebooks, gaming services, or other items that are usually found exclusively online. Click bank is also a great way for smaller internet businesses to take payments without signing up for a more expensive merchant account.

CLICK BOT - A program generally used to artificially click on paid listings within the engines in order to artificially inflate click amounts.

CLICK FRAUD - Clicks on a Pay-Per-Click advertisement that is motivated by something other than a search for the advertised product or service. Click fraud may be the result of malicious or negative competitor/affiliate actions motivated by the desire to increase costs for a competing advertiser or to garner click-through costs for the collaborating affiliate. Also affects search engine results by diluting the quality of clicks.

CLICK STREAM - The order of pages that people are visiting on the site. It is used to indicate what elements of a site are effective, and which are not.

CLICK THROUGH - Term used to measure the number of users who clicked on a specific Internet advertisement or link.

CLICK THROUGH RATE - Commonly abbreviated to CTR, is the percentage of people who click on an advertisement on a particular website. It is a way to measure how successful an online advertising campaign is on a particular website. A high CTR doesn't really reflect sales accurately, only how many people have clicked on the ad. For this reason, most marketers look at the conversion rate instead of the CTR.

CLIENT SIDE TRACKING - Client-side tracking entails the process of tagging every page that requires tracking on the Web site with a block of JavaScript code. This method is cookie based, available as first or third party cookies and is readily available to companies who do not own or manage their own servers.

CO-BRANDING – A term used when businesses emulate other websites by using simil.ar styles of font, graphics and colors, to name a few. This is usually acceptable when the person doing this is an affiliate of the original website, and the method is used to lure customers into the "parent" business.

CLOAKING - Cloaking is a SEO technique where the content that the search engine spiders/crawlers see is different than what's presented to the user. This is achieved by delivering content based on the server's IP addresses. When a user is identified as a spider or crawler then a different version of the webpage is delivered. This is often used in unethical practices normally referred to as "Black Hat SEO". However, it also has some practical purpose to help search engine spiders find content that might be otherwise missed.

CLOSED LOOP MARKETING - Closed Loop marketing is when Marketers focus on finding out what exactly happened to your leads, from start to finish. Closed loop marketing looks at the activities that your leads engaged in to either be converted to customers, or not. This can help Marketing and Sales figure out what activities work in generating sales, and which do not.

COMMENT - The text contained within a "comment" tag in a web page. "Comments" are used in a variety of situations, such as communication between web developers and Cascading Style Sheets.

CMS – Abbreviation for Content Management System is a document centric collaborative application for managing documents and other content. A CMS is often a web application and often it is used as a method of managing web sites and web content.

COMPETITION ORIENTED PRICING - It is a pricing strategy that is based on how the competition is pricing their products. This means if one particular fast-food company is selling their cheeseburgers for a dollar; another might sell theirs for 99c.

CONSOLE – A pop up box that comes up when customers leave a site. The console usually asks customers why they are leaving or if they need any more assistance before moving on to another website.

CONTENT – Content is defined as the actually heart or "meat" of a website, as it offers solid information about something. Text is typically the only element involved in real true content, and can be in the form of a product description, testimonials, company background information, or many other features of a website that give the viewer more insight. Content is the material found in a document or publication. The material can be text, images, video, whitepapers, info-graphics etc.

CONTENT MANAGEMENT SYSTEM - Often abbreviated to CMS, is web application that allows users to add and edit web pages to their websites without having to learn how to use HTML.

CONTENT NETWORK - Also called Contextual Networks, content networks include Google and Yahoo! Contextual Search networks that serve paid search ads triggered by keywords related to the page content a user is viewing.

CONTENT TARGETING - An ad serving process in Google and Yahoo! that displays keyword triggered ads related to the content or subject or context of the web site a user is viewing. Contrast to search network serves, in which an ad is displayed when a user types a keyword into the search box of a search engine or one of its partner sites.

CONTEXTUAL ADVERTISING - Advertising that is automatically served or placed on a web page based on the page's content, keywords and phrases. Contrast to a SERP (search engine result page) ad display. For example, contextual ads for digital cameras would be shown on a page with an article about photography, not because the user entered "digital cameras" in a search box.

CONTEXTUAL DISTRIBUTION - The marketing decision to display search ads on certain publisher sites across the web instead of, or in addition to, placing PPC (Pay Per Click) ads on search networks.

CONTEXTUAL NETWORK - Also called Content Ads and content Network, contextual network ads are served on web site pages adjacent to content that contains the keywords being bid upon.

CONTEXTUAL SEARCH - A search that analyzes the page being viewed by a user and gives a list of related search results offered by Yahoo! and Google.

CONTEXTUAL SEARCH CAMPAIGNS - A paid placement search campaign that takes a search ad listing beyond search engine results pages and onto the sites of matched content web partners.

CONVERSION ACTION - The desired action you want a visitor to take on your site. Includes purchase, subscription to the company's newsletter, request for follow-up or additional search information, lead generation, and download of a company free offer from research results, a video or a tool, and subscription to company updates and news.

CONVERSION – The term conversion means the percentage of people who go from clicking on an ad or visiting a website and actually make a sale. The conversion rate means that the link, ad or site was successful since it moved from a simple click to real, tangible sale.

CONVERSION PATH - It is a method that helps move potential customers to more relevant content. The idea is that customers are provided with a few simple options and they choose whichever one is more relevant to them. Then, based on the customer's choice, more relevant and tailored content is delivered to them.

CONVERSION RATE - It is the number of sales or leads that occur on your website, compared to the total amount of visitors. The term "conversion" refers to the practice of trying to "convert" people from being simply visitors, to being leads or customers. The rate is the percentage of people who you've successfully encouraged to purchase your product or to sign-up for your newsletter etc. Say if you have 10,000 visitors, and 500 of those sign up for your product/service then your conversion rate is 5%. The average conversion rates depend on the industry you're in, but the general consensus is that between 2-3% is good going.

COOKIE - Cookie is a small piece of data that is stored in a user's web browser after they visit a particular site. Every time the user loads the website, the browser sends back the cookie to the website's server with information about the user's previous activity.

COOPERATIVE ADVERTISING - Cooperative advertising is when the costs of an ad are split between two or more businesses. Usually, manufacturers offer this to wholesalers or retailers as a way to encourage them to advertise their product or services.

CO-OP MAILING - The distribution of coupons or other sales promotion offers for a variety of products through a single mailing piece.

COPY TESTING - Sometimes known as "pre-testing" is research into how effective an advertisement is before it goes public. Copy testing looks at consumer feedback, responses and reactions to determine whether the ad is effective or not.

COPYRIGHT - Copyright is the exclusive legal right given to the originator of material to stop people stealing your works. Copyright protects the creator of the material from people who would use their work without permission or acknowledgement. Art, photography, books, music, literature and many more things can be copyrighted.

CORRECTIVE ADVERTISING - If a business runs a misleading advertisement, the Federal Trade Commission may ask them to run another ad (or an ad within the ad). This second "corrective" ad is to correct consumers' mistaken impressions from the first advertisement. An honest and ethical business shouldn't run into such issues.

COST PER ACQUISITION - It is an advertising method where the advertiser only pays for when an advert delivers a sale. Advertiser only pays when the advertising has met its purpose, ensuring that the advertisers don't lose money. This type of advertising is usually only applied to affiliate marketing.

COST PER CLICK (CPC) - It is a strategy that aims to direct traffic to specific websites with ads on other websites. The advertisers pay the website owner every time their ad is clicked on their website owner's page. Cost per click is the amount of money spent to get an advertisement clicked.

COST PER IMPRESSION - Often abbreviated to CPI, is a term used in relation to web traffic. CPI is when advertisers pay each time their ad is displayed to potential customers. It differs from PPC/CPC because the ad doesn't have to be clicked for the advertisers to pay.

COUNTER ADVERTISING - It is an advertising that takes an opposing position to an already-existing advertisement. It is usually seen as an informal response on controversial topics like smoking, unhealthy foods and alcohol.

COST PER ORDER (CPO) - The dollar amount of advertising or marketing necessary to acquire an order. It is calculated by dividing marketing expenses by the number of orders.

COUPON CODE – A special alphanumeric code created by a web merchant's programmer to offer customers. The coupon code is then entered into a special field when the customer places an order. A coupon code is typically for free shipping, a certain percentage off, a gift with purchase, or something similar.

COMPUTREIZED BUYING - The use of computers in managing the purchasing process. Such tasks as calculating current inventory figures, computing economic order quantities, preparing purchase orders, developing requests for vendor quotations, expediting orders, and generating printouts of dollars spent on vendors and products can be part of the system.

CRAWLER – An automated program that many search engines use. The crawler helps to index search terms and web pages into a large directory and tracks progress as well as various statistics to better hone in on how to make the engine more accurate.

CREATIVE DISRUPTION - Creative disruption is when there's a positive change in the normal behavior of a target audience because of a very creative advertisement. Creative disruption is a way of stirring things up for potential customers, who might be ignoring advertisements because of over-saturation and boredom. Creative disruption is definitely a good thing, as you get customers to actually pay attention to your business or product.

CREATIVE STRATEGY - A creative strategy outlines what messages that a business wants to be conveyed about themselves, a particular service or a product. The outlines should also suggest who the message should be directed at and with what type of tone.

CSS – A newer form of html that is short for Cascading Style Sheets. CSS is designed to help separate document content from document presentation. Meaning that the presentation can change background, layout, colors, and fonts while the content of the page stays the same.

CUSTOMER RELATIONSHIP MANAGEMENT - It is the methods and software that helps a business manage their customer relationships. It is all customers' details, such as previous purchases, paid or outstanding bills records, etc that business could keep a database.

CUSTOMER SATISFACTION - It is a measure of how a business's products and/or services have met or surpassed a customer's expectation. 71% of business found that having a way to measure customer satisfaction is a very useful tool in managing and monitoring how well their business is performing.

CTR – A commonly used or seen abbreviation for the term "click thru rate."

D

DAGMAR - It stands for Defining Advertising Goals for Measured Advertising Results. It is when you set goals for an ad campaign so it's possible to figure out if the goal has been met.

DASHBOARD - A monitoring tool that sits on top of a desktop that displays the status of varying metrics, allowing for benchmarking.

DATABASE - A compendium of information on current and prospective customers that generally includes demographic and psychographic data as well as purchase history and a record of brand contacts.

DATABASE MARKETING - An approach by which computer database technologies are harnessed to design, create, and manage customer data lists containing information about each customer's characteristics and history of interactions with the company. The lists are used as needed for locating, selecting, targeting, servicing, and establishing relationships with customers in order to enhance the long-term value of these customers to the company.

DATA SYSTEM - The part of a decision support system that includes the processes used to capture and the methods used to store data coming from a number of external and internal sources.

DECEPTIVE ADVERTISEMENT - A deceptive advertisement is one that can be misleading to consumers. The Federal Trade Committee (FTC) officially states that deceptive advertisement is a "representation, omission, act or practice that is likely to mislead consumers".

DEFAULT PAGE - It refers to the default page setting set to whatever the default (or index) page is in your site's directories. Usually, this will be 'index.html', but on Windows IIS servers, it is often 'Default.htm' or 'index.htm'.

DESCRIPTION TAG - An HTML tag used to provide a description for search engine listings.

DIRECT ADVERTISING - A mass or quantity promotion, not in an advertising medium, but issued from the advertiser by mail or personal distribution to individual customers or prospects. Also, it is the advertising literature appearing in folders, leaflets, throw-always, letters, and delivered to prospective customers by mail, salespeople, dealers, or tucked into mailboxes.

DOMAIN NAME - The address of your website, i.e. www.mybusiness.com

DOUBLE JEOPARDY - It is the evil marketing law that says that small businesses have fewer buyers and less brand loyalty. It's not always the case, but it does happen quite frequently.

DEADLINE – A set time in which ads must be submitted for publication. Can also apply to when articles must be written and submitted, or anything else that has to reach the website designer in time for publicity online.

DEDICATED SERVER – The dedicated server is just that, it serves as the mainframe or server for one particular merchant or website. By using dedicated server, sites stay more stable and emails and other transactions are generally more secure. It also makes websites run generally faster.

DEFAULT – In internet marketing terms, the word default refers to lower paying or more commonly seen ads. When ad space is unsold, often websites will post the default advertising to fill in the space.

DIRECT DIGITAL MARKETING - Direct digital marketing is defined as a digital marketing method that provides relevant marketing communications that are addressable to a specific individual with an email address, a mobile phone number or a Web browser cookie.

DIRECT LINKING – When your affiliate account or program is linked from a banner ad or other online ad, this is known as direct linking. It is not considered to be as effective as using a landing page, but some people still prefer it.

DIRECT MAIL ADVERTISING - The use of the mail delivered by the U.S. Postal Service or other delivery services as an advertising media vehicle.

DIRECT MARKETING – A form of marketing that reaches customers directly. Direct marketing can include emails, postal mail ads, or even phone calls. It is often considered unsolicited since the customer did not request it.

DIRECT RESPONSE - A direct response is when promotions or marketing messages allow or request consumers to reply directly to the advertiser. This can be done through mail, telephone, email or any other form of communication.

DIRECTORY – A list of other websites or services online. The directory is often its own website, edited by humans that contain links to various sources, websites, or other information on a variety of topics.

DIRECTORY SEARCH - Refers to a directory of web sites contained in an engine that are categorized into topics.

DISCUSSION GROUP – The discussion group is a focus group of people who typically communicate via a chat platform to discuss various products or services. Web businesses owners will then use the information or feedback collected from the discussion group to make better decisions or tweak their products in the future.

DISPLAY URL - The web page URL that one actually sees in a PPC text ad. Display URL usually appears as the last line in the ad; it may be a simplified path for the longer actual URL, which is not visible.

DISTRIBUTION NETWORK - A network of web sites (content publishers, ISPs) or search engines and their partner sites on which paid ads can be distributed. The network receives advertisements from the host search engine, paid for with a CPC or CPM model. For example, Google's advertising network includes not only the Google search site, but also searchers at AOL, Netscape and the New York Post online edition, among others.

DOMAIN – A word that points to a website. For example, email users at hotmail.com who have an email address of ***@hotmail.com know that hotmail.com is the domain name. It basically serves as "home base" for email, etc.

DOMAIN NAME - A domain is the main subdivision of Internet addresses, the last three letters after the final dot, and it tells you what kind of organization you are dealing with. There are six top-level domains widely used: .com (commercial) .edu (educational), .net (network operations), .gov (US government), .mil (US military) and .org (organization). Other, two letter domains represent countries; thus;.uk for the United Kingdom, .dk for Denmark, .fr for France, .de for Germany, .es for Spain, .it for Italy and so on.

DOORWAY – A specific web page designed to get more customers. In most cases, the doorway leads to the main product website. An example would be when someone clicks on a large image on a homepage, and then they are taken to a separate page with more details or information. The "doorway" page is designed to entice or invite people to click further and take a closer look at the website.

DOORWAY DOMAIN - A tool used to increase a Web site's position in search engine rankings. The doorway domain page is designed to score well on search engine processes, but the page itself takes users to the main domain when clicked.

DOORWAY PAGE - A web page specifically created in order to obtain rankings within the natural listings of a search engine. These pages generally are filled with keywords and are meant to funnel surfers into the main web site. This practice is generally considered an outdated spam tactic. This term is not to be confused with a "landing page."

DOUBLE LOOP MARKETING - It is the idea that marketing must first start with community, and then move on to commerce. That is first you build up a relationship with your potential customers through sharing information thru blogs, info-graphics, webinars etc. and then only after that will you convert them into paying customers.

DROP SHIPPING – Drop shipping is commonly used when an online merchant does not want to or is unable to store inventory. Instead, the merchant will use a drop shipper who will actually be the source that ships items to customers. Drop shipping makes selling items online easier, since the merchant does not have to keep tract of inventory or acquire new purchases. Instead, all transactions go through the drop shipping company, who then take the order and ship it to the customer.

DUMMY - A preliminary layout for an ad, brochure, poster, or other printed advertising material showing the position and size of the headlines, subheads, body copy, and artwork.

DUPLICATE CONTENT – A term used to describe content that is very similar to other content on a website, or is considered to be unoriginal.

DYNAMIC CONTENT - It is the new content that is being added to your page on a regular basis. Dynamic content usually happens in your blogs, where you can keep updating it with different content that provides your customers with advice and information.

E

E-BOOK – An abbreviation for the term electronic book. EBooks are simply books on a number of different topics that are delivered to customers instantly via email. They can be in several formats including a document or PDF file.

EBUSINESS - A term referring to a wide variety of Internet-based business models. Typically, an e-commerce strategy incorporates various elements of the marketing mix to drive users to a Web site for the purpose of purchasing a product or service.

E-COURSE – Much like an e-book, an e-course is simply curriculum or training which is all electronic or done online. These e-courses can be one time classes to learn a new skill, or they can actually be marketable material to sell to others who want to learn something in particular.

EDGE RANK - It is the common name given to an algorithm that Facebook uses to decide what articles should be displayed on a particular user's news feed.

EIGHTY TWENTY RULE - It means that 80% of a specific product will be sold to about 20% of customers. This usually only applies to a particular product category, for example, shampoo in a drugstore.

ELECTRONIC DATA INTERCHANGE (EDI) - The interfirm computer-to-computer transfer of information, as between or among retailers, wholesalers, and manufacturers.

ELECTRONIC FUND TRANSFER - The use of electronic means, such as computers, telephones, magnetic tape and so on, rather than checks, to transfer funds, or to authorize or complete a transaction. This development has given rise to the concept of the cashless economy.

END USER - This is the person who actually uses a product. This is different from the actual customer, because the end-user doesn't have to actually be the customer. For example, when a person buys a gift for somebody. It's the person who ends up using the gift or usually the person who received the gift that is the end-user.

ENGAGEMENT MARKETING - Sometimes referred to "experiential marketing", "event marketing", "live marketing" or "participation marketing," it is a marketing strategy that tries to fix that which is disconnects, and that can occur between customers and brands by encouraging consumers to participate in the development of a brand. This stops consumers from being passive messengers, and instead taking part in the brand so a relationship grows between the two.

EMAIL - A communication format that involves sending computer-based messages over telecommunication technology. E-mail can include a letter-style text message or more elaborate Web-style HTML messages. Users can also attach other files to the e-mail and transmit all elements simultaneously.

EMAIL MARKETING – Reaching potential and current customers solely via email.

ENTREPRENEUR – The definition of a person who starts their own business, often with money that have out of pocket.

ENTRY PAGE - Refers to any page within a web site that a user employs to "enter" your web site.

EPV – Earnings Per Visitors: A breakdown of how much a website or internet company makes an average based on the number of clicks or visitors it receives.

ESP - Abbreviation for Email Service Provider is a company which offers email marketing and/or bulk email services. They may also provide other services such as email tracking, email segmentation, testing, template creation, subscriber lists etc.

EXIT CONSOLE – A pop up window that comes up as customers are leaving a website. It is often used to get customers' opinions and find out what the web designer can do to improve the site.

EXIT TRAFFIC – Term used to decipher what kind of people or what kind of patterns are taking place when people exit or move away from a website.

EXPIRED DOMAINS – Web domains or domain names that are expired or no longer valid. Email users will get an error message letting them know the domain has expired.

EXPOSURE - Exposure is when consumers have seen or heard a media message. It's doesn't necessarily mean that the consumer has noticed it, only that they were exposed to it. For example, a lot of people will be exposed to a banner ad, but very few will actually pay any attention to it.

EXTERNAL DATA - Data that originate outside the organization for which the research is being done.

EYE TRACKING - Eye tracking is a research method that tracks where a consumer's eyes are focused on. It's often used in marketing to figure out what format works best for advertisements, web pages, blogs etc.

EZINES – Much like an ebook, an ezine is the electronic version of a magazine. Many modern day magazines now supplement their printed version with an ezine and some strictly have the ezine format.

F

FACEBOOK RETARGETING - It is a cookie-based technology that uses an unobtrusive piece of JavaScript coding to anonymously "follow" your audience back to their Facebook after they've visited your website. The coding "learns" what your audience is looking at on your website, and therefore, what they're interested in. This information is then used by marketers to advertise the product/service that the customer was looking at on their Facebook page. Facebook's retargeting can be done through Facebook Exchange (FBX) with their partner programs such as Adroll and Triggit, or with their most recent update, you can now use Website Custom Audience (WCA) directly on their page.

FAVICON – An image use to make a website or online business stand out, such as animated graphics or a logo. A favicon can only be seen by certain browser users. As internet browser users adapt and change, more people will be able to view favicons.

FBX - Abbreviation for Facebook Exchange is a retargeting program that allows marketers to reach people on Facebook who had previously visited their website and shown interest in it. For example, if you visited Resorts.com and searched for resorts in

Singapore but did not make a purchase, marketers can use this information with FBX to send information and advertisements regarding this query to the visitors Facebook page.

FEDERAL COMMUNICATIONS COMMISSION - They're responsible for regulating broadcast and electronic communications.

FEDERAL TRADE COMMISSION - The Federal Trade Commission is responsible for regulating national advertising.

FFA – Acronym for "Free For All," this means exactly what it says: all links, items, or other things on a FFA site are free.

FILTER WORDS – Words that are usually considered junk words, and that do not have much impact on human reaction. Small words used in the English language such as "the," "an," etc are often overlooked and are therefore considered filter words with little to no impact on the marketing of a website.

FIRST PARTY LEADS - It refers to contact information that has been collected directly from the potential customer.

FLASH - It is an animation/interactive platform that allow you to create very complex movements on a webpage. Its most commonly used to distribute videos. For example, YouTube uses Flash.

FLAT RATE – It refers to the very basic rate that is on offer, and there is no option for discounts.

FLIGHTING - This is when the amount of advertisement messages scheduled varies depending on a certain time. For example, 9.00am on a Thursday is a great time to share a new blog post so this is when a business might choose to advertise themselves a lot, where Wednesdays after 8 gets pretty low responses so businesses might not spend much time advertising then.

FOCUS GROUP - It is when a small group of demographically diverse people are brought together and are guided through a discussion about a certain product, service, show etc.

FOUR P's - It refers to Product, Price, Place and Promotion. The product is what you're selling, the price is how much you're selling it at, the place is where you'll be distributing your product and the promotion is how you'll be selling our product.

FORUM – Another term for online bulletin board, a forum is where people can get together and discuss a variety of topics. Forums can be on just about any subject, and today almost every website has forums that they offer to their visitors so they can gather and discuss the topics related to the website.

FORWARDING – Sending email that you received from someone else on to someone from your email address.

FREE BONUS – A term often used to describe a free product or service given to customers who sign up for a service or make purchase. The term free bonus often refers to a month of free service, etc when it comes to internet related merchants.

FREE CLASSIFIED – It refers to a website that offers a free classified advertising. Craiglist.org is a prime example of a free classified website. This is beneficial to those looking to network or meet others online to work together, whether it is through supplying goods or services.

FREE FOR ALL LINKS – Websites that allow people to post their links for free in exchange for their email address. The website owner then sends the person posting the link weekly or monthly advertising emails for their own business. This is highly beneficial Service for both the person posting the free links, and the website owner.

FTP – This is an abbreviation for file transfer protocol. It simply means the transferring of files from your computer directly to your website.

FULL SERVICE AGENCY - This is an agency that handles every part of the advertising process. That includes the planning, design, production, and placement of your ad. Usually it also means that they'll handle all the marketing communication, promotion, sales, PR etc.

G

GENERIC BRAND - It refers to a product that is not connected with a national or private brand name. Some people make the mistake of assuming that "generic brands" do not have a brand at all, but this isn't always true. Usually generic brands do have a brand, but they are just lesser known brands or the store's own brand.

GEO-TARGETING - It is a method of targeting website visitors based on their location or their geography. Once the visitor's location is known, a website might deliver different content based on what country, city, zip code etc. that the visitor is from. It is commonly found in an online advertising. It is also used on internet television platforms in order to restrict certain users from accessing specific content due to digital rights management laws.

GIF – Abbreviation for Graphic Interchange Format. GIF is a graphics format that can be displayed on almost all web browsers. It is a common compression format used for transferring graphics files between different computers.

GOOGLE+ - It is a social networking service provided by Google. Google has describe it as a "social layer" because it also associates web content with that account, i.e. if you comment on a blog, this comment can be made with your Google+ account.

GROSS AUDIENCE - It refers to the total number of audience that you reach in your marketing campaign. As it is a combination of all the different vehicles such as an email, social, blog etc., then sometimes one audience member may be counted twice because they're counted once for each message they receive. For example, if you send an email and share tweets with one particular consumer, they'll be counted twice, once for the email and once for the tweet.

GUERILLA MARKETING – A term used to describe bold and often unconventional forms of advertising and marketing. Often this format can be considered controversial in many cases, but it definitely brings in new customers.

GEO TARGETING - Delivery of ads specific to the geographic location of the searcher. Geo-targeting allows the advertiser to specify where ads will or won't be shown based on the searcher's location, enabling more localized and personalized results.

G.U.I. - Stands for "Graphical User Interface." It means a visual representation of the functional code. Or, is a way for the average web user to interface with a database, program, etc.

GURU – While this term is widely used in many different aspects of life, the term guru in terms of online marketing simply means someone who has a lot of experience and has been successful in the business. Often, people will seek out an internet marketing guru for advice.

H

HEADLINE – The beginning of a business or sales letter is often referred to as the headline. It is without a doubt the most important element of a business or sales pitch since the headline allows the writer to give someone else a good first impression and a bit of background about their business.

HIDDEN TEXT - It refers to the text that is visible to the search engines but hidden to a user. It is traditionally accomplished by coloring a block of HTML text the same color as the background color of the page. Hidden text is also known as Invisible text.

HIT – Another term for clicks, the word hit in internet marketing terms just means how many visits or clicks a website or a particular link receives.

HIT RATE - The percentage of the desired number of outcomes received by a salesperson relative to the total activity level.

HOME PAGE – The main page of a business or a company (i.e. ebay.com or Amazon.com is the company's home page).

HOST – the Company offering to provide bandwidth or hosting for another website.

HOSTING – Actively hosting website. Many online businesses are web hosting businesses. This means they offer their server space or bandwidth to other websites for a monthly fee.

HOT LINKING – Linking up words in another person's site which lead them back to the poster's website. Hot linking is often considered unethical, since the person writing or creating the original content did not authorize the use of the hot links in their writing or site text.

HTACCESS FILE - A file with one or more configuration directives placed in a web site document directory. The directives apply to that directory and all subdirectories.

HTML – In most cases, websites are still written using a coding program called html. Html allows the web designer or programmer to install and place things like form fields, buttons, images, video code, or other items onto a website. Html is a programming language that's used to create websites.

HTML BANNER – It refers to a banner ad using HTML elements to provide interactivity, such as drop-down menus or text boxes, in addition to graphical elements.

HTML EMAIL - E-mail that is formatted using HTML, as opposed to plain text e-mail. Using HTML provides more flexibility with the format and appearance of e-mail, but not all user systems can process it in e-mail.

HTTP - Hyper-Text Transfer Protocol, the format of the World Wide Web. When a browser sees "HTTP" at the beginning of an address, it knows that it is viewing a WWW page.

HTTP REFERRER DATA - A program included in most web analytics packages that analyzes and reports the source of traffic to the user's web site.

HTTPS - Stands for "Hypertext Transfer Protocol Secure."

HYPERLINK - A hyperlink is a word, phrase or image that you can click on to go to another document, page, or place within the same document. They're on most WebPages, making it easy for users to go from page to page. Text hyperlinks are usually underlined and blue.

HYPERTEXT - Any text that that can be chosen by a reader and which causes another document to be retrieved and displayed.

I

IFRAME – It refers to an HTML element which makes it possible to embed another HTML document inside the main document.

IMAGE – The consumer perception of a product, brand, business that may or may not correspond with "actuality."

IMAGE ATTRIBUTION - It is when a credit is given to the creator of an image for their work. A best practice for image attribution is to credit the author's name and then provide a link to their profile, to their original work and to the license deed.

IMPRESSION – The term impression in regards to internet marketing means the exposure of a banner ad or other clickable ad from a website to one individual person.

INBOUND LINK – A link from another website outside of your own website.

INBOUND MARKETING - It is when you promote a business through online content such as blogs, videos, info-graphics, whitepapers, social etc. These activities encourage customers to come in to your business, rather than you going out to talk to them, i.e. prospecting and cold-calling. The content is created in order to create a good relationship between a business/brand and their customers. Inbound marketing takes a lot of dedication and commitment in order to produce a helpful, informative and welcoming business that will hopefully entice customers to find out more about the services/products that are being offered.

INCENTIVE BASED TRAFFIC – Websites that offer compensation for people who visit their site; this is a very popular form of marketing that brings in a large amount of hits. Promotional items such as coffee mugs, calendars, or mouse pads are often given to those who either visit a website or sign up for regular promotional emails.

INCOME REPORT – It refers to a websites' monthly earnings and expenses which typically compiled in a report format.

INDEXED - Google has an index of the web, a kind of like the front of a book has an index of the chapters that the book contains. It keeps things organized and efficient when you go to search a term. You say that a webpage is indexed if it's included in Google's index of the web.

INFOMEDIARY – Term combining information being passed along it at its absolute maximum. The function of an infomediary is to collect or add information to make a website easier to use or more accessible so that more business is being generated.

INFO-PRODUCT – A product that contains primarily information such as an e-book, pamphlet, or other type of information only.

INTERNAL LINK - Internal links are links on a webpage that bring you to another page of the same website/domain.

INTERNET MARKETING - It is just marketing, but on the internet. It is when you, as a business owner or affiliate, use the internet to market a product or service. There's a tonne of methods and strategies that can be employed to do this, from banner ads, blogs posts, PPC, info-graphics, video marketing etc.

INTERSTITIAL – A type of advertisement that expands and can sometimes take up an entire page as a browser visits a site. Often considered a nuisance, this form of advertising is a guerilla style type of marketing that often forces the web surfer to click on it. Interstitial ads that take up a full-screen are called "hyperstitials".

INVENTORY – Whatever an internet merchant or other business owner has in stock. If inventory is low, items can often sell out temporarily until more can be obtained.

IP ADDRESS – A numerical address or series of numbers that identifies each individual computer. These numbers are separated by decimal points. An IP address is much like a telephone number in that it allows all computer users to distinguish and identify each computer.

J

JAVA - Java is an object oriented programming language created by Sun Microsystems that supports enhanced features such as animation, or real-time updating of information. If you are using a web browser that supports Java, embedded in the Web page will automatically run.

JAVASCRIPT - It is a dynamic computer programming language that's commonly used to create interactive effects in web browsers. First developed by Netscape, this popular script program is often seen today on thousands of interactive websites.

JPEG – Acronym for Joint Photographic Experts Group is a graphics format newer than GIF which displays photographs and graphic images with millions of colors, it also compresses well and is easy to download.

JOINT VENTURE – It refers to a business endeavor that combines two or more companies together. A joint venture means that corporations or merchants are joining forces to create a new product, service or website.

K

KERNING - The degree of tightness in the space between type characters such as the individual letters in headlines, subheads, and body copy. Adjusting the degree of closeness between type characters spacing gives the appearance a more natural, readable character.

KEY ITEMS - The items that are in the greatest consumer demand. They are also referred to as best sellers.

KEYWORD – A word used to help give a result for a search. The keyword is also used to integrate into websites and web pages, so that more people look at the page based on those keywords.

KEYWORD DENSITY – How many keywords are in an article published online, or integrated into a web page. A formula is often used to calculate the percentage of keywords to total words written, which is another way to determine keyword density.

KEYWORD MARKETING – A marketing method that is based largely on using keyword dense articles.

KEYWORD PHRASE - A specific word or combination of words that a searcher might type into a search field.

KEYWORD RESEARCH – The word put into finding the right keywords that will bring results for any given online business.

KEYWORDS TAG - A meta-tag used to define the keywords of a Web page for search engines.

KEYWORD TARGETING - Displaying Pay Per Click search ads on publisher sites across the Web that contains the keywords in a context advertiser's Ad Group.

KEYWORD STUFFING - It is the unethical practice of using a keyword or phrase excessively throughout a webpage to falsely increase keyword density. Keyword stuffing can get you banned from the search engines and rightly so. Keyword stuffing is bad and you should avoid it at all costs.

KPI – Acronym for Key Performance Indicators. KPI are metrics used to quantify objectives that reflect the strategic performance of your online marketing campaigns. They provide business and marketing intelligence to assess a measurable objective and the direction in which that objective is headed.

L

LAYOUT - The format of a print advertisement that indicates where the component parts, i.e. artwork, body copy, headline, subhead, trademark, and other graphic elements are to be placed on the page.

LANDING PAGE - It is the page of a website where people have "landed" after clicking a hyperlink on another web page. Every landing page should have one primary objective: To convert visitors into leads. For this reason, there should be a clear CTA on every landing page. There are two basic types of landing pages: Click Through and Lead Gen/Capture pages. The "Click Through" landing page should provide the visitor with more information on the product and/or service. It has a very clear CTA that encourages visitors to click on it, and this usually brings the visitor to a shopping cart or a registration page. A "Lead Gen" or "Lead Capture" landing page usually asks for visitors to share their information. Visitors are encouraged to do so in exchange for something, such as a Webinar, a free eBook or a discount.

LATENT SEMANTIC INDEXING - Often abbreviated to LSI, is an index and retrieval method used by Google and other major search engines. LSI works out what words are related to other words. For example, the word "dress" is related to the word "fashion".

LEAD – A tip or insight into gaining a new business or resource for finding new business. It can also refer to individual people who might be interested in a particular online website or merchant and by finding good leads; the business can fish for new customers.

LEAD GENERATION - The process of collecting contact information and extracting potential sales leads.

LEAD NURTURING - It is when you provide excellent content that's highly relevant, well-researched and very educational to potential customers that are not quite ready to buy. The idea is that this information will "nurture" the relationship with potential customers so that they're aware of your brand, what you offer them and what benefits your services/product provide them with. Lead nurturing ensures that your potential-customers stay emotionally invested in your business, and the only way to do that is to provide those leads with relevant and meaningful content that will hopefully prepare them to make a purchase in the future.

LEAD PRODUCT – A product or item that serves as an introduction to a company and is meant to entice customers who stick around for a while.

LEADING - The amount of space between lines of text on a printed page.

LEAD SALES - The buying organizations that consistently are early adopters of new technologies. Lead users have needs that will become general in the marketplace later on, benefit significantly by obtaining a solution to those needs, and often largely influence other firms' buying decisions. i.e. Intel has been a lead user of microchip production equipment.

LIFE TIME VALUE – An amount of profit a business should expect from one person who becomes a lifelong customer.

LIFESTYLE SEGMENTATION - It is when you separate consumers into different groups, based on their interests, hobbies, and other lifestyle choices.

LIFT LETTER – Commonly mistaken for a sales letter, a lift letter offers customers who have not purchased anything a chance to take advantage of special offers, signup for a month's worth of free services, etc., in hopes to obtain a solid and repeat paying customer.

LINK AUTHORITY - Refers to a type of voting system that happens on your website when another web site links to it. Search engines use these votes in their ranking algorithms, making inbound links great for improving your ranks in search engines.

LINK BAIT - It is a piece of content that you create that attracts a lot of inbound links from other websites.

LINK BUILDING - It refers to the practice of getting other pages, not your own, to link to a page on your website. The practice is used in SEO because Google's crawlers consider links as a type of "vote". So that means the more pages high-quality links linking to your page, the more popular your page is according to Google, and therefore, the more likely it will rank highly in the search engines.

LINK CHECKER – Various software or tools used to verify that links are working properly and leading to valid websites.

LINK EXCHANGE – The process of sharing and exchanging links between websites, people, directories or businesses.

LINK IN - Refers to a social networking platform that is mainly used for professional networking.

LINK POPULARITY – A way to measure how popular and or effective any given link is.

LINK PYRAMID - This is a backlink structure that takes the form of a pyramid. For example, if you imagine that your website is at the peak of the pyramid, and 10 links are pointing back to it, and a different 20 links are pointing to those 10 websites, then 30 other links are pointing towards those 20 and so on and so on. This creates a pyramid structure, with your website at the top.

LINK ROT – Another term for bad link that no longer works or lead to an incorrect or invalid link.

LINK SWAP – It is an exchange of links between websites, individuals or businesses in hopes that each will mutually benefit.

LINK TEXT – The actual text that is showing on the site, which leads people to the link.

LINK VELOCITY - It is the speed at which backlinks to a website are created and/or removed.

LIST – In email marketing terms, a list is simply a compilation of people or email addresses that the sender intends to send marketing emails to.

LOCAL BUSINESS LISTING - A local business listing is a free listing available on search engines that show the physical location of a business on a map, along with other useful information such as phone numbers, websites, opening hours and services. These listings often appear when a user's search query included a specific geographical location. However, if the search query is for a business within your current local area, no geographical term is needed to display the listing locally.

LOCAL SEARCH - A "local search" is the term used for searches that are made for a service/product/store/business etc. that is or will be geographically located close to the internet user's current or intended location. Typical local searches will include a specific location, along with the keyword that the internet user is searching for. For example, "best hotels in Dublin's City Centre".

LOG FILE – It refers to a file that keeps track of activity that occurs on a web server.

LONG TAIL KEYWORDS - Keywords that are longer and more specific keywords that visitors more likely to use when they are close to making a purchase. Long tail keywords generate fewer visitors, but ROI is usually higher because the product is more closely related to the specificities that the consumer was looking for.

LOSS LEADER – Introductory product that is often sold at a loss in the hopes that merchant will gain new business from the customer.

LSI – Acronym for Latent Semantic Indexing. LSI uses word associations to help search engines know more accurately what a page is about.

M

MADE FOR ADSENSE - Abbreviation MFA is used to refer to websites that are built specifically just to make money with the Google Adsense program.

MAILING LIST – It refers to a list that people can opt to be on that will allow them to receive emails weekly, monthly or otherwise. Usually an email mailing list is offered to new subscribers by merchants so they can send them those marketing ads or emails.

MARKETING AUTOMATION - It is a software platforms and technologies that are designed to help marketers and marketing departments and organizations more efficiently and effectively market on multiple online channels, such as websites, emails, social media platforms and email. Marketing automation works by automating certain time-consuming tasks, so that little human error can occur while also ensuring that a regular amount of content is being distributed to target audiences.

MARKETING COMMUNICATIONS - It is the strategy used by a company or individual to reach their target market through various types of communication and marketing messages.

MARKETING RESEARCH - It is the gathering, recording and analysis of data about everything and anything relating to marketing products and services. The purpose of marketing research is to figure out what changing elements of marketing methods effect and impacts customer behavior. There are two types of marketing research, the first is Consumer marketing research, and the second is business-to-business (B2B) marketing research.

MASLOW'S PYRAMID – A model often used in business, created by Abraham Maslow. It basically sections off human needs into five basic categories. Many businesses follow this structure hand in hand with their marketing methods to better identify what people are looking for.

MASTER RESELL RIGHTS – This term refers to people who have full rights to a product, but can also allow others to resell it once they have sold it initially.

MATERIALITY - Materiality is what the FTC says they need to be proven before they regulate a deceptive advertisement. Simply put, the advertisement has to have some serious and material impact on the consumer's decisions or actions in relation to a product or service. If the impact on the consumer is a trivial one, something small and unimportant, then the FTC theoretically will not regulate the advertisement.

MECHANICAL - Also known as a paste-up, it is the final photo-ready assembly of all of the elements of a print ad, brochure, or other printed material that is transmitted to the printer.

MEDIA KIT – Much like a press kit, a media kit contains vital information about a business such as contact information, company logos, websites and links, and basic background of the business like the mission statement. These kits are often used to get more attention or to gain new investors.

MEDIA VEHICLE - It refers to a specific newspaper, magazine, radio station, television program, outdoor advertising location, edition of Yellow Pages, etc., that can be employed to carry advertisements or commercials.

MEMBER'S SITE – A website specially designed for paying or non-paying members. Typically, members' sites give people access to more features and information.

MEME - It is a humorous image, video or piece of text that spreads rapidly across the internet; In the context of web logs, 'blogs, blogging and other kinds of personal web sites it's a kind of list of questions that you saw somewhere else and you decided to answer the questions. This is passed on and repeated as others see them.

MERCHANT - A business unit that buys, takes title to, and resells merchandise.

MERCHANT ACCOUNT – An account merchants can set up that allows them to process and receive credit card payments from customers, whether for individual transactions or recurring billing.

META DESCRIPTION - Refers to the short piece of text that appears in search engine results. It appears at the head section of a webpage. It doesn't influence SEO but including your keyword in the Meta description does increase the likelihood that people will choose to click into your website.

META FEEDS - Ad networks that pull advertiser listings from other providers. They may or may not have their own distribution and advertiser networks.

META REFRESH – It is a way to redirect items within a web browser.

META SEARCH ENGINE - A search engine that displays results from multiple search engines.

METASEARCH ENGINE - A type of Internet search that looks for matches in several search engines simultaneously.

META TAG – A special code or "tag" that contains specific information about inner workings of a web site.

METRICS - A system in SEO that measure the overall traffic, search engine traffic, conversions, top traffic-driving keywords, top conversion-driving keywords, keyword rankings, etc.

MICROBLOGGING - It is a blogging, but smaller in both content and file size. Micro blogs usually let users exchange short or small pieces of content. For Twitter, for example, users can micro blog only 140 characters. Other sites exchange only pictures, or links.

MICRO BUTTON – A very small banner ad on a web page.

MIDDLE OF A FUNNEL - The middle of the funnel occurs after the bottom of the funnel. These are the potential customers that you've engaged successfully enough that they fill out a contact form. This converts them from just a "visitor" to an actual lead. It is important to nurture them by providing them with useful and relevant information, such as blogs, case studies, info-graphics etc. This helps you become a thought leader and a go to for information in your specific industry.

MIME – Acronym for Multi-purpose Internet Mail Extensions, a method of encoding a file for delivery over the Internet.

MOBILE MARKETING - Refers to a marketing directed at your mobile device, such as a smart phone or tablet. Mobile marketing has the benefit of providing consumers with location-based and time-based information that helps to market a product or service.

MODERATOR – Someone in charge of a forum who makes sure that all people posting follow the rules. The moderator is also there to answer peoples' questions and make sure that the forums or bulletin board is running smoothly. A moderator can also be someone in charge of an online chat.

MODEM - It is the device that converts a digital bit stream into an analog signal, and back again, so computers can communicate across phone lines.

MONETIZE - It refers to the process of introducing new features to a website in order for it to make money. This could be a banner ad, affiliate marketing or launching a product or service.

MONEY SITE - Refers to a website where you generate the most amount of your income from.

MOUSETRAPPING – A deceptive method that forces users to view the same page over and over, even after clicking on the backward or forward button within their browser.

MOVABLE TYPE - It means a popular blogging platform.

MPEG – It is the file format that is used to compress and transmit movies or video clips online.

N

NASCENT MARKETS - Refers to small, newly developed markets. Typically, this is the market developmental stage where lots of innovation and competition develops. Usually at this point, the competition is less about brand and image, and more about features and innovations.

NATIONAL BRAND - Refers to a product brand name that is distributed nationally, regionally or locally. It's different from a store brand, which would be a product brand only distributed in that specific store.

NATURAL LISTING - Known as "organic results" or "organic listings" are listings that appear on search engine results page because of their relevance to the searched query/term rather than being advertisements. Think of it as "naturally" appearing, rather than being promoted to appear.

NAVIGATION – A term for the ability to move around online, and to "navigate" a website. If you have advanced navigation skills, you are often savvy about looking up items in search engines, finding information you need, or getting products you want online.

NEGATIVE SEO - Known as "Google Bowling". It's the practice of harming a competitor's website's standing with Google. There's lots of ways to do this, such as hacking a website and putting HTML code with hyperlinks into it, or injecting it with malware – both tactics that would lower a website's Google ranking.

NETIQUETTE – Slang for etiquette online. For example, if you are rude to others via the internet, then you have a bad netiquette.

NETWORK EFFECT – Term for what happens when businesses network, and how they can prosper and see profit.

NEWBIES – This is a term of endearment that refers to people who are new to internet marketing or new to the World Wide Web, or to forums. People who have just signed up to join a forum and begin posting are often referred to as newbies.

NEWSGROUP – An email group that people subscribe to in order to receive news and updates. Many newsgroups send out emails daily, while others opt to send them once a week or even monthly.

NEWSLETTER – Email in newsletter form. Many companies use newsletter format emails to update customers on new products, special sales, and other updates.

NEWS RELEASE – A term for a press release.

NICHE – A specific type of business, i.e. tools or books are considered niche markets. Once you've found a niche, you can then focus on details necessary to become successful in that particular market.

NICHE STRATEGY- A game plan employed by a firm that specializes in serving particular market segments in order to avoid clashing with the major competitors in the market.

NEXT BEST ACTION MARKETING - It is also known as best next action or next best activity marketing, is a strategy that some marketers employ that is extremely personalized to the specific customer. The strategy is a customer-focused marketing tactic that looks at the customer and considers what the next actions that can be taken for them are, and then decides on the 'best' one.

NO FOLLOW LINK - "No-follow" link is an attribute that can be added to the HTML element to instruct some or all search engines that they are not to follow either a specific hyperlink, or all hyperlinks in a page. This ensures that the link target's (the website that you've linked to) ranking will not be affected in the search engine's index. This is usually used if it's not a trusted link, if it's a paid link or prioritizing where you want the search engines to focus on.

NON PROFIT MARKETING - Refers to the service or product that's being offered is not trying to make a profit from what they're offering. Non-profit marketing usually occurs for charities, in the public health sector and educational organizations.

O

O'DESK – It is an online freelance marketplace, a place where businesses can post projects to be worked on by remote workers. It allows employers to organize online work teams, using oDesk team software for management. It can also be used for activities such as worker monitoring or work progress tracking. It lets both parties of a project to have a guaranteed confidence in work and payment done. The site features feedback system for reputation building.

ODD SIZE BANNER – Description of banner ads that take on an unusual size or shape.

OFF PAGE OPTIMIZATION - Refers to the factors that are outside of your control or the control of the coding on your webpage. These factors still have an influence on your web page's listing in search results. You just can't do much about it. An example of off-page optimization is link popularity and page rank: Both of which occur outside of your direct influence.

OFFSITE SEO - Refers to search engine optimization that doesn't take place on your own website. For example, link building or social media sharing.

ON PAGE OPTIMIZATION - It refers to the factors that are controlled by you or by the coding on your page that contribute to having positive effects on how likely it is that your website will rank highly in natural search results. A lot of factors contribute to on-page optimization; a few examples include actual HTML code, Meta tags, title tags, keyword placement and density, outbound links, relevant content and word count.

ONE TIME OFFER – Also known as "up sell" where the customer is presented with an upgrade or deluxe version of the front end product. Typically, one time offers differ from up sells from the way it is viewed. It is only viewable once and the customer may not be able to see the same offer again.

ONE WAY LINK - It is a link that only goes one way, i.e. a link that brings you to a website, but that doesn't provide you with a link back to the original website.

ONSITE SEO - Refers to a techniques that are used by making changes to the website that are supposed to help your website be more search engine friendly.

OPEN GRAPH TAGS - refers to the type of content posted with lots of open graph tags that provide different pieces of information on to Facebook.

OPT IN - When a person "opts in," they're usually making themselves available for communication with you, and/or your business. For example, someone can "opt in" to your mailing list so that you can send them emails.

OPT OUT – The opposite of opt-in, the choice to opt-out means people who have previously signed up for a newsletter, emails, etc are now asking to remove themselves from the list. Another term for unsubscribe.

ORGANIC LINK - It is an inbound link to your website that was created naturally without any persuasion from another webmaster.

OUTBOUND LINK - Refers to a link on your webpage that points to a different website or any page other than your own.

OUTSOURCING – This term means you have chosen to pay others to do the work for you, including shipping and packing items, creating ad content, keeping up the website, or many other duties that are required to have an online business. Outsourcing is similar to having employees, although you simply pay for the outsourcing on a case basis most of the time.

P

PAGE LOADS – Refers to the number of times a page has been viewed. This can easily skew numbers when someone is tracking web hits. If a person is having problems connecting online, they may refresh the same page over and over again, causing a number of page loads that can transfer into hits. It is important to try and find out whether or not a visitor has refreshed a page, or if the page was actually seen by new, unique visitor.

PAGE RANK - Refers to a metric created by Google that determines how much of an authority a webpage is. The metric uses backlinks as the basis for figuring this out. Page rank ranges from 0 as the least authoritative, and 10 as the most authoritative. Page rank is only one of the several ways that Google determines a page's popularity, and trying to improve your page rank in unnatural ways could result in a penalty.

PAGE TITLE - Refers to the title of a webpage. For example, if you have a section for frequently asked questions, the title of this page could be FAQ.

PAGE VIEW – It is when one of your pages of your website is loaded completely, and supposedly "viewed" by a visitor. If one visitor goes to your website and views 3 pages, that's 3 page views.

PAID INCLUSION - It is when a company pays to be included in a search engine company. Paying to be included in a search engine does not mean that you will rank high in that search engine, only that you'll be included in the search engine. Where you rank is still considered an organic result. Paid inclusion programs aren't as popular as they used to be and continue to draw criticism when used.

PANDA - The Google Panda is a series of updates and penalties that was introduced in 2011. Panda targets low quality sites and duplicate content.

PAYPAL – One of the web's most popular sites for accepting payments and receiving payments online. Many merchants opt to use PayPal instead of having a merchant account since PayPal is so widely used.

PAY PER CLICK - Often abbreviated as PPC is an advertising strategy where you pay a certain amount of money for every click your advert on a website receives. It is also known as "Cost Per Click".

PAY PER IMPRESSION – When an advertiser pays for their banner ad to be displayed on a view by view basis, it is otherwise known as a pay per impression.

PAY PER LEAD – Many companies will pay others to find them good leads. Some offer payment on a pay per lead basis, meaning they pay the other party a set rate or amount per lead they receive.

PAY PER POST – Many online marketing gurus think paying people per post on a forum is a great way to generate more revenue. When people see the post, they read the poster's opinion of the product or service, and often seek it out which creates more business.

PAY PER SALE – Often associated with the affiliate programs, a pay per sale program gives people a small percentage of the sales they receive on each item if they are referred.

PAYMENT THRESHOLD - Refers to a minimum commission that an affiliate must accumulate through their earnings before they receive payment. For example, you might have to accumulate $100 before the business will pay you your earnings.

PENALTY - Penalties are incurred through search engine violations. Some of these penalties are automatically given out when spotted by Google's spiders, as they are based on a set of rules programmed into their software. Others are manual, and are based on a human review of a site.

PENGUIN - The Google Penguin is an update and penalty that was introduced in April 2012. Penguin targets unnatural backlinks, which could be from blog spam, paid links, widget bait etc.

PERFORMANCE BASED ADVERTISING – Incentive that pays people based on the actual results they see from the advertising services that they offer. The advertiser or advertising company only gets paid when the company gets business or sales.

PERL – A form of script language that is usually used for developing application programs that work with a web server's CGI functions.

PERMISSION BASED MARKETING - It is when marketers obtain permission from their prospective customers before advancing to the next stage of marketing.

PHP - Also known as "Hypertext Preprocessor" is a widely used programming/scripting language. It is typically embedded into HTML and can be used to create dynamic WebPages. It's also quite popular because it's compatible with many different databases.

PM – Abbreviate for private message, this is usually something sent via an online chat program. In addition, a

PM can be received on a forum, and is only viewable by the user who sent it and the user who received it. Instead of sending email directly to one another, many people chose to use PM instead.

POP BEHIND – When an internet browser clicks on a website, a thread pop up, but remains behind when the user closes his or her browser.

POPULARITY – Another term for ranking a site's success via the number of hits. It also involves a website's search ranking with some of the top search engines such as Google and Yahoo.

PLUGIN - Refers to a bit of software, usually a file or bit of code that can be easily installed another software application to add new feature to it. For example, you might install a plug-in to your browser that can scan for viruses.

POP UNDER - It is a type of online advertisement, banner or webpage that is set to automatically appear underneath the current web browser that the user is using. It's considered an unobtrusive form of advertising because it occurs in behind what the user is doing.

POP UNDER AD – An advertisement that does not pop up, but instead pops underneath the page, so it appears at the bottom when viewed.

POP UP - Refers to an online advertisement, banner or webpage that is set to automatically appear on top of the current web browser that the user is using. It's considered obtrusive as it blocks what the user was doing.

PORTAL – An interactive web tool for registered users to log-in and check things like account information, balances, bills due, past purchases, and other common features.

POSITIONING – Method to get business web page positioned to the top ranking in the search engines in order to gain more business and achieve more hits.

PRE-SELL – Many involved in internet marketing consider it a pre-sell when someone post a positive review or a link to their website without any expenses paid out. Essentially, any free advertising is often considered to be a pre-sell.

PRESS RELEASE – Updated information and or news about a situation or business that is then sent to the press to be publicized in order to reach more people.

PRICING STRATEGY – Tactics used to come up with the best possible price to offer goods and services to customers and clients.

PRIVATE LABEL RIGHTS - Refers to a license given to certain digital products that will allow you to modify, reuse or resell them. The license can be applied to a variety of different products, from ebooks to graphic templates.

PRIVATE SITE – A website that is only viewable and available to paying members. Members usually either pay a onetime fee or a monthly recurring charge in order to remain active and use the website.

Q

QUALIFIED LEAD - It is when you have all the information that you would with a standard lead, such as name and email address, but with additional information that qualifies them for a specific product. For example, you might know what their budget is or whether or not they make the buying decisions in their household/company etc.

QUALITY – A measurement of how well something is received by customers, i.e. a "high quality" product tends to sell much better than one that is low in quality.

R

RANK – How a website measures up against others is called the site rank. It is much like a song on the Billboard top 100 chart; if a website has a higher rank; it is usually seen by more people and is better known.

RATE CARD – Information showing how much advertising costs on particular website. The rate card varies depending on the sponsoring site as well as the ad's size, features, etc.

READER'S DIGEST FORMULA – A marketing method often used when writing articles. Since Reader's Digest is one of the most popular printed magazines ever, many web designers and programmers use the formula to create titles in that very same genre such as "How To", "What Happens" and "Are You" to name a few.

READABILITY - Refers to how easy it is to read a piece of text and for it to be understood.

RECIPROCAL LINK - When someone does something nice for you, it's nice to return the favor; this is exactly what reciprocal links are. When you link to a webpage, they then link back to you.

RECURRING BILLING – Billing to a customer or client that occurs on the same date each month. Basically a monthly fee.

REDIRECT - A redirect is when a visitor, who is trying to go to one specific webpage, is directed towards another one. For example, if a webpage is moved, the owner of the webpage may set it up so that the user it redirected to the webpage's new location.

REDIRECTION – The process of being directed to a different website when clicking on a different link.

REP FIRM – An advertising agency or company who works with a specific company in order to assist them with their marketing needs.

RESIDUAL INCOME – Income that is slowly accumulated and is usually earned through affiliate, the affiliate can then earn residual income as long as the person who signed up continues to pay for that particular service.

RESPONSIVE WEB DESIGN - Also known as RWD, is a method of web designing that aims at creating sites that will provide users with the best possible viewing experience. This usually takes shape in the form of easy reading and navigation with minimum resizing, scrolling and panning. It also means that the web design should be able to be easily viewed on a variety of devices, such as smart phones and tablets.

RETARGETING - Refers to a cookie-based technology that uses an unobtrusive piece of JavaScript coding to anonymously "follow" your audience around the internet after they've visited your website. This is done by placing a piece of coding, sometimes referred to as a "pixel" onto your own website. Every time a visitor browses your websites and leaves without completing a checkout, a browser cookie is dropped. The cookie gives you information that can inform your retargeting provider when and where is appropriate to serve ads/display content as the internet users browses on other sites. This allows for marketers and advertisers to target more specific internet users that are already aware and interested in their business, and provide them with more relevant content that will hopefully get them to make a purchase eventually.

RETURN DAYS – The number of days it takes an affiliate to receive payment from a merchant they are working with once the sale has been made.

RETURN OF INVESTMENT - Often abbreviated as ROI, is the percentage of profit made on the initial investment. For example, if you invested $100 and you earned $150, you're ROI would be 50%.

RICH MEDIA – Online ads that contain motion, sounds, or video and usually use Java or Flash to enhance the viewers experience.

RICH SNIPPET - Refers to the extra bits of text that appear under search results. They are used to mark up specific data, such as an address, phone number or review.

ROBOT – Often also referred to as "BOT", it is software that runs automatically and does not need a human to operate it.

ROBOTS.TXT - Refers to a file or a piece of HTML coding that is usually placed at the start of the directory of your website. The robot.txt file is the first file that crawlers or robots read when they visit the website, as it gives them instructions as to what they can and can't read.

RON – Short for Run of Network, this is an option for ad buyers to place their advertisements on several networked websites.

ROS – Short for Run of Site, this ad buying option allows the buyer to place their ad on various places on one particular website.

RSS - Stands for Really Simple Syndication, is a standard data feed system used to deliver updates and/or content from websites to you, rather than you having to go to the websites looking for them. Popular RSS readers include Google Reader, My Yahoo!, Newsgator and Bloglines.

RSS FEED –This is in reference to a live feed that users can integrate into their email or web browser that allows them to get easy access to live, up to the minute updates in news or other topics that interest them. It can be a handy tool for online marketing. You can encourage visitors to subscribe to your live RSS feed and then update it on a regular basis so that they can see how things are progressing with your website or business.

S

SAFELIST – An email list that people can sign up for to agree to receive email advertisements. Once signed up, the person can also submit their own advertisement, so it is a sort of email marketing network.

SALES FUNNEL - Refers to the processes that a business has set up to increase sales. It contains three major different stages namely: the top, the middle and the bottom. The sales funnel is sometimes seen in a series of WebPages that are designed to get the user to buy a product or service in the end.

SCANNER - An electronic device that records retail purchase data (prices, brands, product sizes, etc.) at the point of sale by means of reading the universal product code.

SCANNING - The process in point-of-sale systems or sale service wherein the input into the terminal is accomplished by passing a coded ticket over a reader or having a hand-held wand pass over the ticket.

SCRAPPING - Web scraping is a technique of extracting information from websites. It's similar to how crawlers work to index pages on the web, except that the focus of scraping is to take unstructured data (usually HTML) and turn it into structure data. The data can then be stored and analyzed in a database or on a spreadsheet.

SEARCH ENGINE – Online tool used to search for terms, information, or other items. Google.com is a prime example of a commonly used search engine.

SEARCH FUNNEL - Movement of searchers, who tend to do several searches before reaching a buy decision that works from broad, general keyword search terms to narrower, specific keywords. Advertisers use the search funnel to anticipate customer intent and develop keywords targeted to different stages. Also refers to potential for switches at stages in the funnel when, for example, searchers start with keywords for a desired brand, but switch to other brands after gathering information on the category.

SEARCH ENGINE MARKETING - Commonly abbreviated to SEM is when search engines are used to market to your target audience. This can happen by using either SEO or by paid methods, such as PPC.

SEARCH ENGINE OPTIMIZATION - Commonly abbreviated to SEO is when your website and online marketing strategy is optimized so that you gain higher rankings in organic search engine results.

SEARCH ENGINE RESULT PAGE - It is the page of results you see after you search something using a search engine, like Google.

SEARCH ENGINE SPAM - Excessive manipulation to influence search engine rankings, often for pages which contain little or no relevant content.

SEARCH SPY - Uninterrupted refreshing page that provides a real-time view of actual Web searches.

SEARCH ENGINE SUBMISSION – Submitting your website's link to a search engine in the hopes that it will appear as a result of your chosen search terms.

SEARCH TERM – Words used to find information via a search engine. For example, if you are looking for fishing tips, the words "fishing tips" are the search term.

SEARCHABILITY - Refers to the ability to be able to pull up information, through an external or internal search engine by using known information, i.e. when someone types in a word, relevant sites will be displayed. To make a website searchable, websites have to contain well-written, relevant and user-targeted content, they have to be accessible and they have to contain related links.

SECURE SOCKETS LAYER – Important tool used to ensure that information is passed from one party to another safety online.

SELF REFLICATING SITE – Websites that appear almost identical, but are offered to affiliates to use in order to market the business. This makes it easier for affiliates to advertise or market the parent business' site while still ensuring that they receive proper credit for any sales that pass through.

SEO – Abbreviation for Search Engine Optimization.

SHARED HOSTING - Refers to a web server that is shared equally with other websites. It's more suited for small sites, but bigger sites need their own individual host.

SHAREWARE - Software free programs that are openly available, and usually they can be downloaded online.

SHOPPING CART SOFTWARE - Refers to a piece of software that is installed on a web servers that allows visitors to select items, and accumulate them in a list, that they intend to eventually purchase. It works the same as a brick-and-mortar shopping cart, except online.

SIG – Abbreviation for signature. This can refer to a signature file, or an email signature.

SIGNATURE FILE – A chunk of text or image at the end of an email that helps to identify the sender. Companies often use their logos as part of their signature file to ensure brand recognition.

SIGNAGE - Banners, billboards, electronic messages, decals, etc., displayed on-site and containing Sponsor ID.

SITE AUDIT - Refers to a full analysis of a site's performance, in order to see if it's meeting a variety of goals. For example, if the goal is to ensure that customers are provided with a fantastic experience of the website, a business might want to ensure that all backlinks are working correctly and that all CTAs are easy to find and understand etc.

SITE LINKS - Site links are hyperlinks to a website's subpages. They appear under certain Google listing and are there to help users navigate easier. The webmaster has no control over site links, but instead Google adds them.

SITEMAP - Refers to a page that links to all other pages on the site allowing spiders to easily find all of the pages on your website.

SITE SEARCH – It refers to a program which provides search functionality specific to one site.

SITE SPEED - Refers to how fast the website loads. the faster, the better.

SKIMMABLE - To make something "skimmable" is to make it easily skimmed, or read through quickly. Bold text, bullet points, short sentences and repetition all help to make a piece of content more "skimmable."

SMARKETING - Refers to a bit of sales, and a bit of marketing. It's the strategic placement of the sales and marketing teams in the hopes that it will be more efficient and profitable.

SOCIAL ADVERTISING - The advertising designed to educate or motivate target audiences to undertake socially desirable actions.

SOCIAL BOOKMARK - It is a backlink to your page that happens when a user pastes a link to your site publicly, for example on Reddit or Pinterest.

SOCIAL MEDIA - Social media can come in a variety of shapes and sizes. It can be a platform, website or application, and it is distinguished from other websites etc. because it is used for social interactions. An example of this is Facebook, Twitter and Instagram.

SOCIAL MEDIA MARKETING - Refers to social media platforms, such as Facebook, Twitter and Instagram, which are used to garner interest in a business and to increase website traffic. Social Media Marketing usually focuses on sharing interesting content that users will want to share with their friends, who will then share with other friends etc.

SOCIAL SHARE - Social sharing is when a visitor to your website shares your webpage on social media. For example, clicking the "like" button and posting to Facebook or "pinning" something to Pinterest.

SOCIAL SIGNALS - Refers to an SEO measurement that happens outside of your website. It determines the popularity of a specific webpage based on how many times it has been shared, liked and discussed on social media sites.

SOLO ADVERT – An advertisement that stands on its own, such as an entire welcome video on a homepage, a commercial, or some other format of ad that does not rely on network but instead serves its purpose on its own, usually on the brand or company's own homepage.

SPAM - Refers to those annoying unsolicited emails you get that clog up your inbox. It's also applied to unhelpful or unproductive comments or duplicate or repeated submissions to blogs, forums or any public platform. Unwanted, unsolicited e-mail, typically of a commercial nature.

SPAMDEX – Index providing people with information on companies who tend to send spam.

SPIDER - Also known as a "crawler" is a piece of software that is used to crawl the internet and index data appropriately; Software that is automated and runs through search engines in order to index web pages into search engine.

SPINNING - Spinning is when you take a piece of content and put a new perspective on it, making it a new article.

SPLIT RUN – When the same ad is sent to different websites but has varying wording or headlines, this is known as a split-run.

SSL – Abbreviation for Secure Sockets Layer

SPLIT TESTING - Split testing happens when you test different versions or changes on web page to see which one does better. The performance is usually measured by looking at the click through rate or return on investment. Common things that are split tested are headlines, images, copy, layout and design.

SQUEEZE PAGE - In the digital world, a highly targeted list of email subscribers allows the owner to market his product and service with a fairly high probability of success. However, with the proliferation of spam, consumers are very careful about giving out their email addresses. To ease consumer concerns, experienced online businesses create "Squeeze Pages" that detail what the subscriber will be receiving and the business' privacy standards. Businesses that responsibly use "Squeeze pages" have experienced substantial boosts in the visitor-to-subscriber conversion rates.

STICKINESS - In internet marketing it usually used to refer to content and to websites that are often revisited and re-read by users. Content that's sticky might be something that a user can return to time and time again, like a useful guide or an extensive resource list. A website that is sticky might have a useful tool, such as a Title Generator.

SUBSCRIBER - Refers to a user who has agreed to be contacted by you with regards your business. Agreed is the key word here. If they haven't agreed, they're not subscribing. If you email them anyways, you're spamming them.

SUBMISSION –The process of entering information into a form and then sending it via the web to a server.

SUBMIT – A common tag on buttons at the bottom of forms for people making a submission.

T

TAGS - Refers to a keyword or term that's associated with a piece of information or content, such as an image, a blog or an internet bookmark. A tag helps to describe the item and allows it to be found easily by browsing the term or keyword that's been associated with it. Tags are usually chosen informally and personally by the creator of the content or information, or by the viewer, depending on the context. For example, many blogs will allow users to attach tags to their blog posts so that the blog will be easily found through those tags. They're also quite popularly used for events, where a specific tag can be used by everyone in connection with images, presentations, comments and articles related to the event.

TARGETED – Advertising geared toward a person or group of people who would most likely buy a particular good or service. This can refer to all forms of marketing, as long as it is designed to reach a specific group of customers.

TARGET AUDIENCE - Refers to your target audience is a specific audience that you think will buy your product. It's usually based off of specific demographical information, such as age, gender and income.

TARGET MARKET - Refers to a group of people that you intend to aim your marketing message at.

TARGETING - Narrowly focusing ads and keywords to attract a specific, marketing-profiled searcher and potential customer. You can target to geographic locations, by days of the week or time of day, or by gender and age (demographic targeting). Targeting features vary by search engine. Newer ad techniques and software focus on behavioral targeting based on web activity and behaviors that are predictive for potential customers who might be more receptive to particular ads.

TELESCOPE TEST – A method of determining which ads are being the most effective in order to maximize profit or productivity.

TEMPLATE – A standard set of files with images and headers that are already in place. All the advertiser has to do is insert their own words or image into the template, save it, and publish online.

TESTIMONIAL – A quote or review submitted by customers who are impressed with a business goods or services. Testimonials are designed to lure more customers in by reading what other customers have to say about the company.

TEXT AD – Ad online advertisement that is strictly text; no graphics, sounds or animation are used.

TEXT LINK EXCHANGE - A network where participating sites display text ads in exchange for credits which are converted into ads to be displayed on other sites.

THEMES - A theme is an overall idea of what a web page is focused on. Search engines determine the theme of a web page through analysis in the algorithm of the density of associated words on a page.

THUMBNAIL - A rough sketch of the layout for a piece of print advertising.

TITLE TAG - Tag of a web page that contains the page title. The page title should be determined by the relevant contents of that specific web page. The contents of a title tag for a web page is generally displayed in a search engine result as a bold blue underlined hyperlink.

TLD - Stands for Top-Level Domain is the name that appears along with the 2nd dot in a website's address.

For example, in www.example.ca, ".ca" is the TLD. Other common TLD's are .com, .net and .org.

TLP – Stands for Top Level Page, a reference to the home page, category pages, or product pages that have unique value for the site and so are structured in the top levels of the site directory.

TLP FEED - Acronym for Top Level Page feed, the often automatic and on-subscription feed of an advertiser's home page or unique category pages.

TOP OF FUNNEL - Refers to the first stage that you come in to contact with your consumer. It is the largest part of the sales funnel, because you have the most people coming in before they make up their minds whether to make a purchase with you or not. For example, those who click on a banner ad and are brought to the website would be considered at the "top of the funnel". It isn't until the consumer chooses to be contacted by you that they are converted into the "middle of the funnel".

TOP OF MIND AWARENESS - It is when a business, brand or specific product is the first to come to a consumer's mind when thinking of a particular industry. For example, if you're thinking the technology industry, the brand that might come into your mind is Apple.

TOP SITE – When web site is ranked high, it is then dubbed a "top site."

TRACKBACKS - A protocol that allows a blogger to link to posts, often on other blogs, that relate to a selected subject. Blogging software that supports Trackback includes a "TrackBack URL" with each post that displays other blogs that have linked to it.

TRACKER - A model using three waves of survey data to predict 12-month test market sales for a new consumer nondurable product. The approach views potential customers as proceeding sequentially through stages of awareness, initial product trial, and repeat purchase. The overall prediction of sales over time is constructed by predicting the time trend of these three quantities (awareness-trial-repeat) using the survey data.

TRACKING – Methods used to keep an eye on ads, who views them, how many people viewed them and how many of those clicks generate sales.

TRACKING CODE - It is a snippet of JavaScript that is copied and pasted from your Google Analytics account on to your website. It's used by Google Analytics to track data from a website and it usually starts with <script> and ends in </script>.

TRACKING URL - A specially designed and/or unique URL created to track an action or conversion from paid advertising. The URL can include strings that will show what keyword was used, what match type was triggered, and what search engine delivered the visitor.

TRAFFIC – The term used to describe activity on World Wide Web. Refers to the number of visitors a website receives. It can be determined by examination of web logs.

TRAFFIC ANALYSIS - The process of analyzing traffic to a web site to understand what visitors are searching for and what is driving traffic to a site.

TRICK BANNER - A banner ad that attempts to trick people into clicking, often by imitating an operating system message.

TRUSTED FEED - It is also known as Paid Inclusion, a trusted feed is a fee-based custom crawl service offered by some search engines. These results appear in the "organic search results" of the engine. Typically, the fee is based on a "cost per click," depending on the category of site content. It has been called a "Trusted Feed" due to the ability to actually alter the content in the feed, without changing the existing website.

TWITTER - Refers to a social networking service that has been described as "texting for the internet". Users can send and receive text messages, called "tweets," that are 140 characters long.

TWITTER RETARGETING - Refers to a cookie-based technology that uses an unobtrusive piece of JavaScript coding to anonymously "follow" your audience back to their Facebook after they've visited your website. The coding "learns" what your audience is looking at on your website, and therefore, what they're interested in. This information is sent from the website to the retargeting provider where they connect the information with the correct Twitter account and advertise relevant content.

TWO TIER – Term used to describe an affiliate program that allows the affiliate to generate revenue or commission from sales, but also from referring new affiliates as well.

TXT – Text file.

TXT AD – text ads as mobile device text messages.

U

UCE – Short for Unsolicited Commercial Email, this is another term for Spam.

UNCLAIMED DOMAINS – Websites or .com address that has not yet been used claimed, or that have no activity there.

UNIQUE – Distinction between visitors; each click has its own unique footprint, and each person has a different IP address, so gauging the uniqueness of each hit is imperative to accurate track results.

UNIQUE USERS - The total number of different users, or different computer terminals which have visited a Web site. This is measured using advanced tracking technology or user registration.

UNIQUE VISITOR – Term to describe an individual hit to a website by each unique IP address. A measurement of Web site traffic that reflects the number of individuals who have visited a Web site (or network) at least once during a fixed time frame.

UNSOLD INVENTORY – Stock or inventory that still remains unsold.

UNTARGETED – Niche markets that may not have been reached yet through advertising; businesses can benefit greatly from looking for new, untargeted audiences who may be interested in their services or products.

UP SELL – Process of selling a lead product, and then trying to get the customer to buy another item or upgrade the item to a more expensive one.

URL – Abbreviation for Uniform Resource Locator. It is the internet address for a specific webpage or a definition of a particular location or web address on the internet. Term is often used interchangeably with domain and Web address.

USABILITY - Web usability is the ease in which you can use a website. Usability is often related to the presentation of information; design, easy to understand information, clear options and choices and key terms placed in appropriate areas. Another element of usability refers to how easy content and websites are easy to view and use on various devices and browsers.

USENET – Refers to a helpful tool that compiles information on the web; for use in newsgroups, websites or other resources.

USP – Abbreviation for Unique Selling Preposition. This term refers to ways a company can offer unusual or unique benefits to customers, and then using that information to gain new clients.

V

VERTICAL BANNER –A banner ad that runs on a website vertically instead of horizontally, usually on the side of the page to the right; a banner ad measuring 120 pixels wide and 240 pixels tall.

VIRAL CONTENT - When content is shared and shared and shared and shared; and shared once more, all super quickly. It gets its name from the speed that a virus would spread, i.e. really quickly.

VIRAL MARKETING – Form of marketing that infiltrates as many different avenues as possible, usually in the form of videos, cell phone transmissions, or posted on various forums in order to get more exposure.

VIRUS - These are programs that can be downloaded onto your computer or network from the Internet. Some are harmless, others are programmed to destroy your system, trash your files and disable your software. Use anti-virus programs to take extra protection.

VIRTUAL HOSTING – A form of web hosting that is not done on one single server but instead is running websites from several different computers.

VLOG - A vlog is a video blog.

VIRTUAL PRIVATE SERVER - Commonly abbreviated as VPS, A virtual server usually running Windows or Linux that you can remote into. Most SEO's use a VPS to run link building software uninterrupted or to host websites depending on your goal.

VISIT - In internet marketing context, refers to when a user visits your website.

VISITOR QUALITY – A way to determine the actual interest of visitors visiting a particular site. This can help to gauge the success of the ad or website, and the potential for profit.

W

WEB 2.0 - It describes the websites that are more complicated than the static pages that were first prevalent in earlier websites. There wasn't one particular update that was the cause of the new name, but it was a bunch of changes in the way web pages were coming to be made and used. Features of Web 2.0 tend to have a social element to them, such as: Blogs, networking sites, wikis, video sharing, web applications, social media platforms etc.

WEB ANALYTICS - The process of using web metrics to extract useful business information.

WEBINAR - It comes from the term "web" and "seminar" and that's pretty much exactly what it is. A webinar is an online event hosted by a company/organization that's broadcasted to a group of individuals who have opted in to hear/watch the broadcast via their computers. The webinar is run by a moderator, usually a representative of that company/organization and occurs through the use of a web conferencing tool. There are usually two components to a webinar: Visual and audio. Guests of the webinar can watch PowerPoint presentations, videos, WebPages or any other visual medium that the moderator decides will be useful to the viewers. While the guests watch the visuals, the moderator can also talk about the topic, and they can also receive questions.

WEB BROWSER – A program that allows people to use the internet, i.e. Firefox, Netscape, and Internet Explorer are all examples.

WEB DESIGN – The process that goes into creating websites is known as web design.

WEB DIRECTORY – An online directory of various websites usually relating to one particular topic or divided up into various categories so visitors can easily find sites they need.

WEB DIRECTORY - An organized, categorized listings of Web sites.

WEB HOST – Provider of memory, storage, and connectivity in order to post a live website.

WEB MASTER - The individual assigned to administering a corporation or organization's web site.

WEB PAGE - A HTML (Hypertext markup Language) document on the web, usually one of many together that make up a web site.

WEB RING – A way to navigate a large number of websites that are closely related simply by clicking forward or backward within the web ring.

WEB SERVER – The actual physical computer that holds and stores the information and memory needed to host websites.

WEB SERVER LOGS - Most web server software, and all good web analytics packages, keep a running count of all search terms used by visitors to your site. These running counts are kept in large text files called Log Files or Web Server Logs. Useful for developing and refining PPC campaign keyword lists.

WEBSITE - Refers to a place, with one or more pages, on the internet; a collection of interconnected electronic "pages" available on the Internet used to provide information about a company, organization, cause or individual.

WEBSITE TRAFFIC - Any of a number of measures to describe the amount of visitors and vists a Web site receives.

WEBSITE USABILITY - The ease with which visitors are able to use a Web site.

WEB TV - Television set-top boxes that allow users to browse the Internet from their televisions without a computer system.

WHITE HAT SEO - Also called "Ethical SEO", white hat SEO refers to the optimization techniques that focuses on the actual people and visitors of the website (as opposed to the crawlers) and completely follows search engine rules, guidelines and policies. A website that is optimized for search engines but focuses on providing visitors with relevant content and organic ranking is considered to be using white hat SEO. Other examples of white hat SEO is keywords, link building and link popularity.

WHOIS This website lets you see who the owner of a website is, where the domain is registered, and contact information of the owner. This is an excellent tool for helping to find or prevent fraud as well.

WIDGET - A widget is a live update on a website, webpage, or desktop. Widgets contain personalized neatly organized content or applications selected by its user.

WIKI - A web application that allows users to add content, as on an Internet forum, but also allows anyone to edit the content. Wiki also refers to the collaborative software used to create such a website.

WIKIPEDIA - A multilingual, web-based, free content encyclopedia project. Wikipedia is written collaboratively by volunteers from all around the world. With rare exceptions, its articles can be edited by anyone with access to the Internet, simply by clicking the edit this page link. Since its creation in 2001, the name Wikipedia is a portmanteau of the words wiki (a type of collaborative website) and encyclopedia.

WORD COUNT - The total number of words contained within a web document.

WORD OF MOUTH ADVERTISING - Refers to an advertising that happens when people share information about a product, service or promotion with friends or family or anyone. According to a recent Nielson study, it's still the most trusted form of advertising, with 92% of people saying they trust it.

WORDPRESS – A very popular and user friendly program that gives novices a chance to publish and write the blog itself into a website that the owner creates.

WORLD WIDE WEB - A portion of the Internet that consists of a network of interlinked Web pages. This is the aspect of the Internet most familiar to users.

X

XML - Stands for "Extensible Markup Language," a data delivery language.

XML FEEDS - A form of paid inclusion in which a search engine is fed information about an advertiser's web pages via XML, rather than requiring that the engine gather that information through crawling actual pages. Marketers pay to have their pages included in a spider-based search index based on an XML format document that represents each page on the advertiser site. Advertisers pay either annually per URL or on a CPC basis - and are assured of frequent crawl cycles. New media types are being introduced into paid inclusion, including graphics, video, audio, and rich media.

XML MAPS - XML maps are specially formatted links to your pages. They will never replace the need for HTML site maps.

XML SITEMAP - Refers to a list of pages on your website. The Sitemaps provide webmasters with an easy way to tell search engine robots about pages on their websites that are available for crawling, that the robots might not find by themselves.

Y

YAHOO – Popular portal, search engine, and email host on the web.

YOUTUBE - Refers to a video-sharing website, created by three former PayPal employees in 2005. It was bought by Google in 2006. It's a powerful marketing tool with 50% of people watch videos on YouTube, with 64% of those going to the marketer's website afterwards.

Z

ZINE – It is an abbreviation for magazine. It refers to magazines that are published digitally rather than on paper. Some are mainstreams; others are oddball and cover almost every topic imaginable.

ZIP - A method of file compression originally used with MSDOS and a file extension for files that are zip compressed.

ABOUT THE AUTHOR

Kim Faith is the founder of URBAN Design LLC. She is an Architect by Profession. Resided in Guam USA for three years and later transfer and resided to Singapore for twenty three years. She traveled mostly mainly due to her architectural works, places namely Tokyo, Hokkaido, Sapporo in Japan; Malaysia; Indonesia; Korea; Hongkong; Alaska; Los Angeles; Vancouver in Canada, Seattle in Washington, Philippines; and stayed for a year in Sakhalinsk's Yuzno in Russia for Sakhalin Energy Project. She loves staying all her spare time searching for something to learn, read and study at the National Library of Singapore.

The author is a member of Shekinah Four Square Church in Singapore.

ONE LAST THING...

If you enjoyed this book or found it useful, chances are that your friends will too.

I'd be very grateful if you'd post a short review on Amazon. Your support really does make a difference and I read all the reviews personally so I can get your feedback and make this book even better.

Thanks again for your support!